ATION

WONDER

THE NATURAL HISTORY MUSEUM POETRY BOOK

NATURAL
HISTORY
MUSEUM

WONDER

THE NATURAL HISTORY MUSEUM POETRY BOOK

CHOSEN BY

ANA SAMPSON

MACMILLAN CHILDREN'S BOOKS

Published in association with the Natural History Museum, London

The galleries and exhibits at the Natural History Museum are constantly being updated and refreshed.
Some of the exhibits mentioned in this book may not be on display right now.

Published 2021 by Macmillan Children's Books
an imprint of Pan Macmillan
The Smithson, 6 Briset Street, London EC1M 5NR
EU representative: Macmillan Publishers Ireland Ltd, 1st Floor,
The Liffey Trust Centre, 117–126 Sheriff Street Upper,
Dublin 1, D01 YC43
Associated companies throughout the world
www.panmacmillan.com

ISBN 978-1-5290-5899-4

1 3 5 7 9 8 6 4 2

A CIP catalogue record for this book is available from the British Library.

Printed and bound by CPI Group (UK) Ltd, Croydon CR0 4YY

To my amazing little sister – and the scientist of the family –
Caroline. My hero, and everyone else's.

Contents

'We Are Volcanoes' – Earth   **45**

'Listening to the trees' – Plants   **53**

'Hurt no Living Thing' – Creepy Crawlies 135

'How heavy is a whale's dream?' – Mammals   **159**

'How doth the little crocodile / Improve his shining tail' – Reptiles

'Our footprints' – Human Evolution and Biology   **221**

Introduction

The Natural History Museum in London's South Kensington welcomes over five million visitors in a normal year to marvel at the treasures housed in its twenty-eight galleries. Less than 1% of the Museum's collections of over eighty million objects is on display at any one time. Behind the scenes stand kilometres of preserved specimens, libraries of rare books and artworks, wonders gathered on some of the most famous voyages in history, rooms packed with pressed plants and stuffed animals, and freezers full of DNA. As well as a Museum, it is a state-of-the-art centre for discovery hosting over three hundred resident scientists and over ten thousand visiting researchers each year, who investigate everything from dinosaurs to life on other planets.

The Natural History Museum's collections began life as part of the holdings of the British Museum, which was founded when Sir Hans Sloane (1660-1753), President of the Royal Society and the man we have to thank for bringing drinking chocolate to Britain, sold his library and specimens to the British government for a generous price. When Sir Richard Owen became the superintendent of the natural history collections in 1856, he realized that they needed more space and began campaigning for a new site. Transporting the collections took more than a year and the zoological treasures alone required nearly four hundred journeys across London by horse and cart – which must have been quite a sight! The beautiful, richly decorated Victorian building was designed by the relatively inexperienced architect Alfred Waterhouse as a cathedral to nature, conceived to inspire a love for the natural world – and it is no less awe-inspiring now than when its doors first opened on Easter Monday 1881.

VIEW OF CENTRAL HALL.

'I live on a small star which it is my job to look after' – Behind the Scenes at the Museum

Anyone visiting the Natural History Museum will find themselves marvelling at the variety, the beauty and the strangeness of the abundance of life on our planet – and beyond. With wonder comes the desire to preserve our world's fragile ecosystems and protect the amazing plants and animals that thrive in them. The Museum's collections enable scientists from across the globe to study many areas such as biodiversity, crop diseases, rare species and the biggest threat that everything on the planet faces: climate change. The Museum's vision is of a future where people and planet can thrive, and its mission is to create and inspire passionate advocates for the planet who will work towards that goal.

Behind the Scenes at the Museum

There's a fellow down in fossils, in his life he's dug down deep.

There's an elderly explorer – plans expeditions in her sleep.

There's a butterfly pursuer, now cocooned in his duvet.

Eyelids flutter as he dreams of the ones that got away.

There's a woman, feeling frantic she's busy making lists

and packing bags and making notes of the things that she might miss.

And others have set off – with the whole world to explore.

So much has now been found, but they know that there is MORE!

It's time for sifting sands or shifting stones to find those bits and bones

or packing plants, observing ants in a team, or all alone.

They add to our understanding to our hopes and to our dreams.

They are part of background work going on behind the scenes.

The coveting, collecting, the studying, the dating

the display, the presentation, the recording, the collating.

Some travel far. Some stay at home – *their* forest is one of books.

They leaf through them, think them through and offer us a look.

Some peer through a microscope, note data, wonder, hope.

And why?

So that we can pop in – anytime we like –

Taking a break from our all-too-normal life.

We can muse and we can wander – worlds laid out for us to see.

And we can wonder, gasp, sigh and dream. . .

. . . and be back home in time for tea.

Michaela Morgan

Order on the Phone to a Large Department Store

Could I order an explosion
please. As large as they come
and quite fantastic.
Would you make it out to
my account; I want it now,
to collect, not posted.
It has to happen immediately,
at once, or the whole thing's
wasted. And when I see it,
for the price they charge,
I want it large, large.
With fantastic colours shooting
out of the flames, and the loudest
"bang of all bangs".
No-one will be hurt; just shaken
and astonished. Not shocked
in the medical sense,
just jolted hard
so that life takes a different angle
and a totally new,
refreshing direction.
After all it will be a huge explosion.

Sally Heilbut

Who cares
if we poison the land,
the seas? We fell all the forests,
we topple the trees? There's plenty
more galaxies, planets like these — with
water, with air, with warmth, with light:
homes like ours just right for life. Who cares
if we lose those buzzy old bees? Who cares
if there's plastic clogging the seas? When
our blue world is finally done, we'll leave
this rock and mother sun, we'll zoom
on up - to way out where - there's
many more earths. . . .
or are there?

James Carter

The Holocene Extinction

When we began, our feet trod lightly
Bare upon the earth, we were weightless
Travellers, allowing resurgence and
Regrowth, leaving enough.
Reverence.

Forging through millennia, we kept on
Adding endless weight, leadening
Heaviness, leaving deep and lasting
Indentations, sending shockwaves.
Eliminating.

Cruelty, cavernous greed, no impediment,
Hands and feet became Industrial.
Monsters, spewing toxicity, sickening,
Deafening, echoing arrows.
Piercing.

Now thundering, trampling boundlessly.
Decimating pathways once bountiful.
We watch helplessly, numb, aching,
Hollow, haunting cries in empty spaces.
Waiting.

Stop. I hear hope, purposely striding.
Footsteps pleading necessary action.
Great minds whirring, channelling change,
Demanding, respectfully our weight to
Lessen.

I want birdsong, abundant fluttering,
Humming, no more poison, destruction.
Growing for growth, it has to end.
Will my generation see the rightful
Rising?

Dara McAnulty

A Small Star

I live on a small star
Which it is my job to look after;
It whirls through space
Wrapped in a cloak of water.

It is a wonderful star:
Wherever you look there is life,
Though it's held at either end
In a white fist of ice.

There are creatures that move
Through air, sea and earth,
And growing things everywhere
Make beauty from dirt.

Everything is alive!
Even the very stones:
Amazing crystals grow
Deep under the ground.

And all the things belong,
Each one to the other.
I live on a precious star
Which it is my job to look after.

Gerard Benson

#ExtinctionRebellion

The day will come when papers
will only tell leaf-stories
of blackbirds' quarrels with sparrows.

Their pages will roll back into trees
and the front page will be bark.

Tabloids will be hundred-winged birds
singing earth anthems.

I'll settle into the buttress root of my armchair
and watch ants swarm

to text me secrets from the soil
adding emojis
of all our lost species.

I'll be surrounded by phones
that light up with chlorophyll,
vibrating like workers in their hives –

an apiary of apps.

I'll touch a vanda orchid
and it'll open
easily as hypertext,

everyone will hold leaves
intently as smartphones

to hear them retweet birdsong
from archives.

This is my homepage, where I belong.
This is my wood wide web,

my contour map
with which to navigate
a new internet –

rootlets sparking towards rootlets
underground.

Underground
where resistance is in progress –

fungal friends working in darkness,
their windows blacked out.

Pascale Petit

Invisible Magicians

Thanks be to all magicians,
The ones we never see,
Who toil away both night and day
Weaving spells for you and me.

The ones who paint the rainbows
The ones who salt the seas
The ones who purify the dew
And freshen up the breeze

The ones who brighten lightning
The ones who whiten snow
The ones who shine the sunshine
And give the moon its glow

The ones who buff the fluffy clouds
And powder blue the skies
The ones who splash the colours on
The sunset and sunrise

The ones who light volcanoes
The ones who soak the showers
The ones who wave the waves
And open up the flowers

The ones who spring the Spring
And warm the Summer air
The ones who carpet Autumn
And frost the Winter earth

The ones who polish icicles
The ones who scatter stars
The ones who cast their magic spells
Upon this world of ours

Thanks to one and thanks to all
Invisible and true
Nature's magic heaven sent
To earth for me and you.

Paul Cookson

from Mont Blanc

The fields, the lakes, the forests, and the streams,
Ocean, and all the living things that dwell
Within the daedal earth; lightning, and rain,
Earthquake, and fiery flood, and hurricane,
The torpor of the year when feeble dreams
Visit the hidden buds, or dreamless sleep
Holds every future leaf and flower;—the bound
With which from that detested trance they leap;
The works and ways of man, their death and birth,
And that of him and all that his may be;
All things that move and breathe with toil and sound
Are born and die; revolve, subside, and swell.

Percy Bysshe Shelley

All Nature Has a Feeling

All nature has a feeling: woods, fields, brooks
Are life eternal: and in silence they
Speak happiness beyond the reach of books;
There's nothing mortal in them; their decay
Is the green life of change; to pass away
And come again in blooms revivified.
Its birth was heaven, eternal is its stay,
And with the sun and moon shall still abide
Beneath their day and night and heaven wide.

John Clare

'The same stream of life'

The same stream of life that runs through my veins
night and day runs through the world and dances
in rhythmic measures.

It is the same life that shoots in joy through the
dust of the earth in numberless blades of grass and
breaks into tumultuous waves of leaves and flowers.

It is the same life that is rocked in the ocean-cradle
of birth and of death, in ebb and in flow.

I feel my limbs are made glorious by the touch of
this world of life. And my pride is from the life-
throb of ages dancing in my blood this moment.

Rabindranath Tagore

The Tables Turned

An Evening Scene on the Same Subject

Up! up! my Friend and quit your books;
Or surely you'll grow double:
Up! up! my Friend, and clear your looks;
Why all this toil and trouble?

The sun above the mountain's head,
A freshening lustre mellow
Through all the long green fields has spread,
His first evening yellow.

Books! 'tis a dull and endless strife:
Come, hear the woodland linnet,
How sweet his music! on my life,
There's more of wisdom in it.

And hark! how blithe the throstle sings!
He, too, is no mean preacher:
Come forth into the light of things,
Let Nature be your Teacher.

She has a world of ready wealth,
Our minds and hearts to bless –
Spontaneous wisdom breathed by health,
Truth breathed by cheerfulness.

One impulse from a vernal wood
May teach you more of man,
Of moral evil and of good,
Than all the sages can.

Sweet is the lore which Nature brings;
Our meddling intellect
Mis-shapes the beauteous forms of things: —
We murder to dissect.

Enough of Science and of Art;
Close up those barren leaves;
Come forth, and bring with you a heart
That watches and receives.

William Wordsworth

Finding Magic

Are you looking for magic?
It's everywhere.
See how a kestrel
Hovers in air;
Watch a cat move:
What elegant grace!
See how a conker
Fits its case.
Watch a butterfly come
From a chrysalis,
Or a chick from an egg—
There's magic in this;
Then think of the
Marvellous mystery
Of an acorn becoming
A huge oak tree.
There's magic in sunsets
And patterned skies:
There's magic in moonlight—
Just use your eyes!
If you're looking for magic
It's easily found:
It's everywhere,
It's all around.

Eric Finney

Atlas

Give him strength, crouched on one knee in the dark
with the Earth on his back,
                            balancing the seven seas,
the oceans, five, kneeling
in ruthless, empty, endless space
                            for grace
of whale, dolphin, sea-lion, shark, seal, fish, every kind
which swarms the waters. Hero.

                            Hard, too,
heavy to hold, the mountains;
burn of his neck and arms taking the strain –
Andes, Himalayas, Kilimanjaro –
give him strength, he heaves them high
to harvest rain from skies for streams
and rivers, he holds the rivers,
holds the Amazon, Ganges, Nile, hero, hero.

Hired by no one, heard in a myth only, lonely,
he carries a planet's weight,
                            islands and continents,
the billions there, his ears the last to hear
their language, music, gunfire, prayer;
give him strength, strong girth, for elephants,
tigers, snow leopards, polar bears, bees, bats,
the last ounce of a hummingbird.

Carol Ann Duffy

On the beach at night alone

On the beach at night alone,
As the old mother sways her to and fro singing her husky song,
As I watch the bright stars shining, I think a thought of the clef of
the universes and of the future.
A vast similitude interlocks all,
All spheres, grown, ungrown, small, large, suns, moons, planets,
All distances of place however wide,
All distances of time, all inanimate forms,
All souls, all living bodies though they be ever so different, or in
different worlds,
All gaseous, watery, vegetable, mineral processes, the fishes, the
brutes,
All nations, colors, barbarisms, civilizations, languages,
All identities that have existed or may exist on this globe, or any
globe,
All lives and deaths, all of the past, present, future,
This vast similitude spans them, and always has spann'd,
And shall forever span them and compactly hold and enclose
them.

Walt Whitman

Being but men

Being but men, we walked into the trees
Afraid, letting our syllables be soft
For fear of waking the rooks,
For fear of coming
Noiselessly into a world of wings and cries.

If we were children we might climb,
Catch the rooks sleeping, and break no twig,
And, after the soft ascent,
Thrust out our heads above the branches
To wonder at the unfailing stars.

Out of confusion, as the way is,
And the wonder, that man knows,
Out of the chaos would come bliss.

That, then, is loveliness, we said,
Children in wonder watching the stars,
Is the aim and the end.

Being but men, we walked into the trees.

Dylan Thomas

A pen and ink sketch of the obelisk raised at the landing site of the
Wold Meteorite in Yorkshire

'I could not sleep for thinking of the sky' – Space

The natural world extends far beyond the earth's stratosphere, and in the Museum's galleries visitors can learn about all aspects of the cosmos, from asteroids to solar flares and even the possibilities of life on other planets. The Museum's collections boast moon rock samples, meteorites and even a smudge of microscopic diamonds formed in the dust of dying stars *billions* of years before our solar system even existed.

Among the Museum's amazing exhibits from space are the Wold Cottage meteorite, which was seen plummeting to earth by a surprised Yorkshire farmer in 1795, and the enormous iron Campo del Cielo meteorite, which landed in Argentina a few years ago. Many of these fascinating artefacts have been put to practical use to expand human knowledge of what lies beyond our skies. For example, in 2006 the Museum allowed NASA to break open a piece of the Nakhla meteorite, which fell from Mars, in order to investigate its core. It contains traces of fire opals – and scientists believe that if microbes have ever existed on Mars, traces of them might be preserved in opal deposits on the planet's surface.

The Point

Point to the sky.
Draw a line from your finger.
It'll go on forever.
Through light and through darkness.
Past astronauts sleeping.
Past clouds and past planets.
Through silence unmeasured.
Through time uncounted.
A line that's so long.
It will never stop going.
Long after you've dropped
your hand to your side.
And gone back indoors.
That line is still sketching.
Onwards and outwards.
Universe threading.
Oh, your finger's a marvel.
Take care where you point it.

A. F. Harrold

The Unending Sky

from Lollingdon Downs

I could not sleep for thinking of the sky,
The unending sky, with all its million suns
Which turn their planets everlastingly
In nothing, where the fire-haired comet runs.
If I could sail that nothing, I should cross
Silence and emptiness with dark stars passing;
Then, in the darkness, see a point of gloss
Burn to a glow, and glare, and keep amassing,
And rage into a sun with wandering planets,
And drop behind; and then, as I proceed,
See his last light upon his last moon's granites
Die to a dark that would be night indeed:
Night where my soul might sail a million years
To nothing, not even Death, not even tears.

John Masefield

Cosmic Disco

Rocking-with-wind-trees
waltzing-with-moon-ocean –
Everything in purposeful motion
like the lifting lark
or the swirls of Saturn

Even the far-away stars
explode
on the dance-floor of infinity –
grouping and regrouping
into new constellations.
O see them
under the shifting disco
of the inter-galactic lights –

The gravitational boys
in their shimmering shirts.
The orbiting girls
in their luminous glad-rags –
within magnetic reach of their rotating handbags.

Grace Nichols

Solar System Candy

If I ate the solar system,
the moon would taste
strange and dusty
as Turkish Delight.
Planets would be
giant gobstoppers,
except Saturn and Jupiter –
those gas giants
fizz like sherbet,
or melt like candy floss
in your mouth.
The meteor belt
pops and crackles
like space dust.
Comets leave a minty sting
on your tongue.
Black holes taste of cola bottles.
Or memories
you once had
and lost.

Gita Ralleigh

Excursion to the Planet Mercury

certain evenings a little before the golden
foam of the horizon has properly hardened
you can see a tiny iron island
very close indeed to the sun.

all craters and mirrors, the uncanny country
of the planet Mercury – a mystery
without I without air,
without you without sound.

in that violently magic little place
the sky is racing along
like a blue wrapper flapped and let go
from a car window.

now hot now cold
the ground moves fast,
a few stones frisk about
looking for a foothold

but it shales it slides
the whole concept is only
loosely fastened
to a few weak tweaks of gravity.

o the weather is dreadful there:
thousand-year showers of dust
all dandruff and discarded shells
of creatures too swift to exist:

paupers beggars toughs
boys in dresses
who come alive and crumble
at the mercy of metamorphosis.

no nothing accumulates there
not even mist
nothing but glimmering beginnings
making ready to manifest.

as for the catastrophe
of nights on mercury,
hiding in a rock-smashed hollow
at about two hundred degrees below zero

the feather-footed winds
take off their guises there,
they go in gym shoes
thieving and lifting

and their amazed expressions
have been soundproofed, nevertheless
they go on howling
for gladness sheer gladness

Alice Oswald

The Way Planets Talk

What might we hear if we listened
for the star-forged language
the planets used when sound was new
and words had no full stops?

We might hear the distant vowels
of Neptune, each word as long
as life, each sun-abandoned syllable
the sound of a breathing whale.

We might hear the soft lilt of Uranus,
with its dictionary of duck eggs
plopped into blue flour – a thousand
definitions in a single air-thrown sigh.

We might hear the singing voice of Saturn,
with its billion letter alphabet
scattered along a single groove,
its voice recorded in a tantrum of sentences.

We might hear the whirling words of Jupiter,
where 'hello' is the oil in an engine
and 'I love you' is the red echo
of a candle flame dying at sunrise.

We might once have even heard Mars
utter its own name before the words dried
on the tip of its burnt tongue, before
a final, thirst-silenced cry scratched the dust.

We might hear Venus,
Venus who speaks in a dialect
separated from our own
only by a dream on a too-warm night.

And nestled between stone-fist silences
we might hear Mercury
wailing like a boiled baby
each time the sun scrubs its face.

If we listened we might hear these planets,
and take the language from their molten cores
and learn that distance is a comma,
a pause in how we talk about tomorrow.

Dom Conlon

Moons

Some people think of moons as children,
Eagerly racing but never straying
Far from their parent's side.

But really they are the mums,
They are the dads and their
Lives shrink whilst yours swells.

They watch volcanoes erupt,
Storms rage, ice creep and
Sunlight shine across your surface.

Mostly they stay quiet and close,
Guiding your tides and doing their best
To catch any meteors which might hurt you.

Then, at night, as half your face
Lies against its pillow, they tuck you in
And glow with pride.

Dom Conlon

Meeting An Astronaut

Science Museum
Autumn Half-Term

He stands there proudly
 in his NASA spacesuit
  in front of
   his lunar module

He talks
 of moonwalking
  and earthgazing

He speaks
 of the silence
  and the strangeness
   of space

He confesses
 some part
  of him
   will always
    drift about
     up there
      in that big
       black nothing

Though the module
is only a model,
the astronaut
only an actor –
playing his part
saying his lines
time after time

Yet still
we walk away
all starry-eyed

James Carter

To the Evening Star

Thou fair-hair'd angel of the evening,
Now, whilst the sun rests on the mountains, light
Thy bright torch of love ; thy radiant crown
Put on, and smile upon our evening bed !
Smile on our loves, and while thou drawest the
Blue curtains of the sky, scatter thy silver dew
On every flower that shuts its sweet eyes
In timely sleep.   Let thy west wind sleep on
The lake ; speak silence with thy glimmering eyes,
And wash the dusk with silver.   Soon, full soon,
Dost thou withdraw; then the wolf rages wide,
And the lion glares thro' the dun forest :
The fleeces of our flocks are cover'd with
Thy sacred dew : protect them with thine influence.

William Blake

Twinkled to Sleep

Cerulean night-sky
    Star-set;
Stygian-dark river-plain
East, north, west,
    Dance-set;
Myriad amber-flashing
Lights dancing, rays flashing, all night.

Delight! delight! Inexpressible heart-dance
    With these.
Strange heart-peace, in sparkling lights!
Blithe heart-ease, starry peace, dancing repose!
Star-charmed, dance-enchanted eyes close,
    Appeased.

Dance in jet-dark depth, in star-set height,
Lights dancing, west, east,
Star-high, heart-deep,
    All night.

Ursula Bethell

Dazzle Dance

I am made of heat and light
comets spinning through the night
spit and splinter – meteorite
firecracker, pinwheel bright.

I am made from ash and coal
watch my embers wax and glow
twist and turn my body so
dragon breath to volcano.

I have frazzle crackle hands
dance a razzle dazzle dance
simmer swirling twist and prance
glitter, sparkle to entrance.

I am made of cinder stars
gasses burning from afar
supernova in the dark
flash of thunder full of spark.

I incinerate and blaze
candles burning in my gaze
born of fire, heat and flame
come and bask beneath my rays.

Sue Hardy Dawson

Comet

(To be read as quickly as possible, in as few breaths as you can manage.)

I'm a spinning, winning, tripping, zipping, super-sonic ice queen:
see my moon zoom, clock my rocket, watch me splutter tricksy space-steam.

I'm the dust bomb, I'm the freeze sneeze, I'm the top galactic jockey
made (they think) of gas and ice and mystery bits of something rocky.

Oh I sting a sherbet orbit, running rings round star or planet;
should I shoot too near the sun, my tail hots up: *ouch – OUCH – please fan it!*

And I'm told I hold the answer to the galaxy's top question:
that my middle's made of history (no surprise I've indigestion)

but for now I sprint and skid and whisk and bolt and belt and bomb it;
I'm that hell-for-leather, lunging, plunging, helter-skelter COMET.

Kate Wakeling

Let Them Eat Chaos

Picture a vacuum

An endless and unmoving blackness

Peace

Or the absence, at least
of terror

Now,
in amongst all this space,
see that speck of light in the furthest corner,
gold as a pharaoh's deathbox

Follow that light with your tired eyes.
It's been a long day, I know, but look —

watch as it flickers
then roars into fullness

Fills the whole frame.
Blazing a fire you can't bear the majesty of

Here is our Sun!
        And look – see how the planets are dangled around it
                and held in their intricate dance?
        There is our Earth.

Our
        Earth.

                                        Kae Tempest

Blazing in Gold and Quenching in Purple

Blazing in Gold and quenching in Purple
Leaping like Leopards to the Sky
Then at the feet of the old Horizon
Laying her spotted Face to die
Stooping as low as the Otter's Window
Touching the Roof and tinting the Barn
Kissing her Bonnet to the Meadow
And the Juggler of Day is gone.

Emily Dickinson

A view of the crater of Mount Vesuvius, Italy, before the great eruption of 1767

'We Are Volcanoes' – Earth

The Natural History Museum has over 180,000 specimens of minerals and rocks and they come from all over the planet – and, in the case of the meteorites and moon rocks – far beyond. These samples can tell us much about our world. For example, the stripes on a large chunk of 2.5-billion-year-old banded iron show us how bacteria in the seas began to produce oxygen that made the earth's atmosphere welcoming to early life-forms. A sample of granite collected on Scott's famous trek to Antarctica enabled scientists to learn all sorts of interesting things about the make-up of that mysterious continent. The Museum also houses samples of jadarite, a new mineral discovered in 2006 which has a chemical composition almost identical to that quoted in the film *Superman Returns* for Superman's nemesis: 'kryptonite'.

The Museum boasts a collection of glamorous gemstones and priceless treasures, including the huge, sparkling blue Ostro stone, from the Amazon rainforest. This enormous cut topaz weighs over two kilograms – a little heavy for a necklace! Many of the Museum's jewels and rocks are still housed in the original oak display cabinets in which they amazed and delighted the first visitors to the Museum in 1881.

Prometheus Amid Hurricane and Earthquake

Earth is rocking in space!
And the thunders crash up with a roar upon roar,
And the eddying lightnings flash fire in my face,
And the whirlwinds are whirling the dust round and round–
And the blasts of the winds universal leap free
And blow each other upon each, with a passion of sound,
And æther goes mingling in storm with the sea!

Aeschylus

The Museum's famous earthquake simulator allows visitors to experience what it would have been like to feel the 1995 Kobe earthquake that devastated part of Japan's Hyōgo Prefecture. Visitors can stand in the aisles of a recreated supermarket and be wobbled by the strong tremors that shook the ground for around twenty destructive seconds, watching the products on the shelves shudder and fall.

We are volcanoes

after Ursula K. Le Guin

There may be quiet years,
years when it seems
they are mountains again,
and mountains bring awe
in their way but you get used
to seeing them in one frame,
expect them always to be
the same fertile ground
for foot-worn paths,
loose-soiled slopes
that need mapping.

There may be quiet years,
when the hardened crust
is cool to the touch and
it seems you could dig
and find only rock and ash –
and maybe the fossils
of more dangerous things.

There may be quiet years
when the plates shift a little,
and the mountain shakes –
some smoke, some heat
but life carries on the same,
no urgency –

do people not know what it means
when a mountain moves?

There may be quiet years
but this is not one of them

Jo Brandon

A still—Volcano—Life—

A still—Volcano—Life—
That flickered in the night—
When it was dark enough to do
Without erasing sight—
A quiet—Earthquake Style—
Too subtle to suspect
By natures this side Naples—
The North cannot detect
The Solemn—Torrid—Symbol—
The lips that never lie—
Whose hissing Corals part—and shut—
And Cities—ooze away—

Emily Dickinson

An emerald is as green as grass

An emerald is as green as grass;
A ruby red as blood;
A sapphire shines as blue as heaven;
A flint lies in the mud.
A diamond is a brilliant stone,
To catch the world's desire;
An opal holds a fiery spark;
But a flint holds fire.

Christina Rossetti

The Quercus Oak, which is also depicted in panels
on the Hintze Hall ceiling

'Listening to the trees' – Plants

Comprising over six million botanical specimens, the Museum's collections of herbs, ferns, lichen, algae, seeds and even slime moulds from every continent on earth are world famous. Some of the samples were gathered as long ago as the seventeenth century – and by some of the world's most renowned explorers and scientists, including Captain Cook and Charles Darwin.

Researchers at the Museum study plants from everywhere in the world, looking at the amazing diversity of earth's flora, the diseases that might threaten it and the possibilities of new food crops.

Think of it

Think of it

The first shudder of damp
That somehow signaled
All was ready

Then
In the deep inside of earth
In the muted underneath of winter
Spring began

Not with a sudden trumpet of green
Or a sky of confetti blossoms
But with a seed
Small, pale and barely breathing

It lay quietly
Waiting for the lavender clouds
That carry the first warm rains

Then
For some reason as ancient and
Everyday as the sun itself

The seed cracked
Split and softly burst into
A faint tendril
A root a sprout
A thin wisp of a growing thing

And
With no thought of stopping
It pushed through the
Dark soil with the force of
A billion winter winds
Until it

Pierced the crust of the outside and
Split the frozen armor of earth

Which has held spring safe
Since time began

Zaro Weil

from The Desire of Life

But in the earth remains the Seed,
springtime's forgotten, hidden treasure.
Memories of seasons, visions of life,
ghosts of a world, its base and its tenor –
the Seed embraces them all, beneath dead earth
and thick fog, a shield against Winter's icy spectre.
It grips Life in all its thrumming joy
and bears the promise of Spring's green wonders.
It dreams of birdsong in flight,
the juice of a fruit, the scent of a flower.

Abu Al-Qassim Al-Shabbi
translated from the Arabic by Ali Al-Jamri

Plant a Tree

He who plants a tree
    Plants a hope.
    Rootlets up through fibres blindly grope;
Leaves unfold into horizons free.
    So man's life must climb
    From the clods of time
    Unto heavens sublime.
Canst thou prophesy, thou little tree,
What the glory of thy boughs shall be?

He who plants a tree
    Plants a joy;
    Plants a comfort that will never cloy;
Every day a fresh reality,
    Beautiful and strong,
    To whose shelter throng
    Creatures blithe with song.
If thou couldst but know, thou happy tree,
Of the bliss that shall inhabit thee!

He who plants a tree,—
    He plants peace.
    Under its green curtains jargons cease.
Leaf and zephyr murmur soothingly;
    Shadows soft with sleep
    Down tired eyelids creep,
    Balm of slumber deep.

Never hast thou dreamed, thou blessèd tree,
Of the benediction thou shalt be.

He who plants a tree,—
   He plants youth;
   Vigor won for centuries in sooth;
Life of time, that hints eternity!
   Boughs their strength uprear;
   New shoots, every year,
   On old growths appear;
Thou shalt teach the ages, sturdy tree,
Youth of soul is immortality.

He who plants a tree,—
   He plants love,
   Tents of coolness spreading out above
Wayfarers he may not live to see.
   Gifts that grow are best;
   Hands that bless are blest;
   Plant! life does the rest!
Heaven and earth help him who plants a tree,
And his work its own reward shall be.

Lucy Larcom

Pear Tree

Silver dust
lifted from the earth,
higher than my arms reach,
you have mounted.
O silver,
higher than my arms reach
you front us with great mass;

no flower ever opened
so staunch a white leaf,
no flower ever parted silver
from such rare silver;

O white pear,
your flower-tufts,
thick on the branch,
bring summer and ripe fruits
in their purple hearts.

H. D.

One of the Museum's most iconic architectural elements is the beautiful ceiling in Hintze Hall. A riot of plants – including lemons, pears, oranges, cherries, apples, tobacco, poppies, figs, olives, vines, sunflowers, rhododendrons, irises, nutmeg, tea and oak – range over one hundred and sixty-two gorgeously painted panels. Originally, artists painted directly onto the plaster. In 1975, the panels were restored to their full gleaming glory.

Roots and Leaves Themselves Alone

Roots and leaves themselves alone are these,
Scents brought to men and women from the wild
    woods and pond-side,
Breast-sorrel and pinks of love, fingers that wind
    around tighter than vines,
Gushes from the throats of birds hid in the foliage of
    trees as the sun is risen,
Breezes of land and love set from living shores to you
    on the living sea, to you O sailors!
Frost-mellow'd berries and Third-month twigs offer'd
    fresh to young persons wandering out in the
    fields when the winter breaks up,
Love-buds put before you and within you whoever
    you are,
Buds to be unfolded on the old terms,
If you bring the warmth of the sun to them they will
    open and bring form, color, perfume, to you,
If you become the aliment and the wet they will
    become flowers, fruits, tall branches and trees.

Walt Whitman

Counting-Out Rhyme

Silver bark of beech, and sallow
Bark of yellow birch and yellow
    Twig of willow.

Stripe of green in moosewood maple,
Color seen in leaf of apple,
    Bark of popple.

Wood of popple pale as moonbeam,
Wood of oak for yoke and barn-beam,
    Wood of hornbeam.

Silver bark of beech, and hollow
Stem of elder, tall and yellow
    Twig of willow.

Edna St Vincent Millay

Ash-boughs

Not of all my eyes see, wandering on the world,
Is anything a milk to the mind so, so sighs deep
Poetry to it, as a tree whose boughs break in the sky.
Say it is ash-boughs: whether on a December day and furled
Fast or they in clammyish lashtender combs creep
Apart wide and new-nestle at heaven most high.
They touch heaven, tabour on it; how their talons sweep
The smouldering enormous winter welkin! May
Mells blue and snow white through them, a fringe and fray
Of greenery: it is old earth's groping towards the steep
  Heaven whom she childs us by.

Gerard Manley Hopkins

The Redwoods

Mountains are moving, rivers
are hurrying. But we
are still.

We have the thoughts of giants –
clouds, and at night the stars.

And we have names – guttural, grotesque –
Hamet, Og – names with no syllables.

And perish, one by one, our roots
gnawed by the mice. And fall.

And are too slow for death, and change
to stone. Or else too quick,

like candles in a fire. Giants
are lonely. We have waited long

for someone. By our waiting, surely
there must be someone at whose touch

our boughs would bend; and hands
to gather us; a spirit

to whom we are light as the hawthorn tree.
O if there is a poet

let him come now! We stand at the Pacific
like great unmarried girls,

turning in our heads the stars and clouds,
considering whom to please.

Louis Simpson

Redwoods and Sequoias share many characteristics but, although Redwoods can grow taller, the Sequoia is the biggest tree on earth in terms of the volume and circumference of their huge trunks. The slice of a giant Sequoia Tree exhibited in the Natural History Museum came from an enormous, ancient tree that was a seedling in the year 557. Before it was felled in 1893 – a task that took two men more than a week – it had been growing for 1,300 years in the Sierra Nevada Mountains in California to reach an astonishing height of over 90 metres – taller than the Museum itself. The amazing Sequoia can flourish for up to three thousand years.

Listening to the trees

And the birch says
    it's about dancing and colour

and the rowan says
    it's about berries and birds

and the willow says
    it's about shape and shelter

and the hazel says
    it's about love and lichen

and the aspen says
    it's about growth and the wind

but I say it's about
    listening to the trees

Mandy Haggith

On Forgetting That I Am a Tree

A poem in which I am growing.

A poem in which I am a tree,
And I am both appreciated and undervalued.

A poem in which I fear I did not dig into the past,
Did not think about my roots,
Forgot what it meant to be planted.

A poem in which I realise they may try to cut
    me down,
That I must change with the seasons,
That I do it so well
It looks as if they are changing with me.

A poem in which I remember I have existed
    for centuries,
That centuries are far too small a unit of
    measurement,
That time found itself in the forests, woods
    and jungles.
Remember I have witnessed creation,
That I am key to it.

A poem in which some will carve their names
    into my skin
In hopes the universe will know them.
Where I am so tall I kiss the sun.
Trees cannot hide,
They belong to the day and to the night,
To the past and the future.

A poem in which I stop looking for it,
Because I am home.
I am habitat.
My branches are host and shelter.
I am life-giver and fruit-bearer.
Self-sufficient protection.

A poem in which I remember I am a tree.

Ruth Awolola

Mushrooms

Overnight, very
Whitely, discreetly,
Very quietly

Our toes, our noses
Take hold on the loam,
Acquire the air.

Nobody sees us,
Stops us, betrays us;
The small grains make room.

Soft fists insist on
Heaving the needles,
The leafy bedding,

Even the paving.
Our hammers, our rams,
Earless and eyeless,

Perfectly voiceless,
Widen the crannies,
Shoulder through holes. We

Diet on water,
On crumbs of shadow,
Bland-mannered, asking

Little or nothing.
So many of us!
So many of us!

We are shelves, we are
Tables, we are meek,
We are edible,

Nudgers and shovers
In spite of ourselves.
Our kind multiplies:

We shall by morning
Inherit the earth.
Our foot's in the door.

Sylvia Plath

Waterlily

glory be to the *näckros*, naked rose,
open rose, white flower of water.

glory be to water, held in dropped-
stone-ripple, thickened to the green

pad of a leaf. & in time
let us praise the spread

of all anchored things.
praise to the long pale roots

& the chain of water. & let us
take this flower, its quiet face

on the surface & its searching
root as the mystery of faith.

glory be to the work of the pond
& to silt, to the white

open flower which is an offering
& will be given up for us.

Seán Hewitt

Fern

Fern's first form is furled,

Each frond fast as a fiddle-head.

Reach, roll and unfold follows.
      Fern *flares*.

Now fern is fully fanned.

Robert Macfarlane

Fern

What I love about ferns	are their fronds.
What I love about ferns	are their shapes.
What I love about ferns	are the way their new fronds curl up tightly.
What I love about ferns	are the way their fronds unfurl.
What I love about ferns	is that they can live for 100 years.
What I love about ferns	is that they've been on this planet for 360 million years.
What I love about ferns	is that they can live together in a fernery.
What I love about ferns	is the way they stroke the trunks of trees on the forest floor.
What I love about ferns	is that they can clean polluted air.
What I love about ferns	is their names —
common staghorn fern,	bird's nest fern,
hart's-tongue fern,	liquorice fern,
ostrich fern,	interrupted fern.

Chrissie Gittins

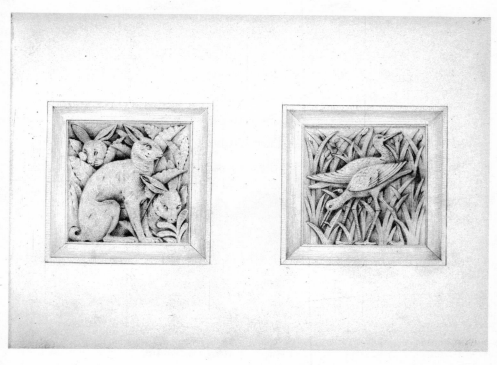

Designs for the Natural History Museum featuring birds and hares, by Alfred Waterhouse (1830-1905)

One of the most interesting and charming elements of the Museum's architecture is the presence of hundreds of carvings – of birds, beasts and plants, including lots of luxuriant ferns – that climb up and cling to its walls and columns. The Museum's founder Sir Richard Owen provided specimens and diagrams to architect Alfred Waterhouse so that Waterhouse could design terracotta sculptures that were lively, beautiful and factually accurate. Extinct plants and animals can be found adorning the east wing, and living flora and fauna the west.

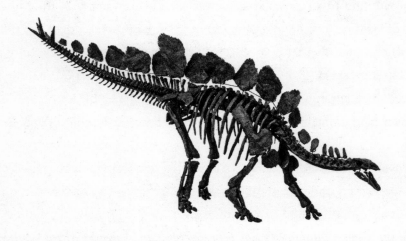

Stegosaurus stenops

Reconstructed Stegosaurus specimen, discovered in Wyoming, USA, 2013. The Stegosaurus lived around 150 million years ago, in the late Jurassic period. This specimen, on display in the Natural History Museum, is the most complete Stegosaurus skeleton in existence.

'Dinosaurs Walked Here' – Fossils and Dinosaurs

The dinosaur and fossil galleries are a star attraction to many of the Museum's millions of visitors. In fact, it was the Museum's first superintendent, Sir Richard Owen, who coined the name dinosaur, which means terrible or fearfully great lizard. The dinosaurs – of which more than a thousand species have been discovered so far, ranging from the size of a humming bird to some of the largest ever land animals – dominated our planet for 160 million years.

We learn about dinosaurs from fossils, which are formed when an animal's remains are buried under many layers of mud or sand. Over time – sometimes thousands or millions of years – compression of the remains turns them into sedimentary rock. Humans had been finding fossil evidence for dinosaurs including bones, teeth, tracks, eggs and even droppings for millennia, but nobody knew what they were. For example, a *Megalosaurus* bone discovered in seventeenth century Oxfordshire was, at various times, supposed to have come from a giant or a Roman war elephant. A rash of discoveries in the early nineteenth century prompted Sir Richard Owen to identify this strange new group of animals and we still have much to learn about them today, including discovering what finally drove them to extinction.

A Real Live Fossil

What was it like, back at the beginning of you?

Before dust,
before the fire finished time's slow work,
before the museum,
before we pieced you together, all of your puzzle-parts,
before we named you, brand new: *swift–footed lizard.*

What was it like, back before I found you?
And before the days before I found you?
Before the boulder cracked like an egg
and spilled your secrets.

What was it like before that?
Before the glacier scooped you up
and carried you along,
all those years and miles away.

Were you waiting?

Before you stripped down to bare bones,
before you laid down on the ground for good,
before your
very
      last
           day.

And all the days before that — what were they like?

Back at the beginning of you,
when you first stepped, unsteady,
out on to the earth?

Rachael M. Nicholas

The Natural History Museum's 'Dippy' is perhaps the world's most famous dinosaur cast. The first bone of this enormous sauropod was found in Wyoming in 1898. It took three years to painstakingly uncover enough bones to reconstruct a full *Diplodocus* skeleton and thirty-six packing cases to transport casts of all of the 292 bones to London. In 1905, the Museum's replica was unveiled at a grand ceremony attended by the cream of London society.

Diplodocus

The replica skeleton of Diplodocus carnegiei was presented to the Museum in 1905 by Andrew Carnegie

Dippy has had a few homes, including taking pride of place in Hintze Hall as the awe-inspiring first sight greeting visitors to the Museum between 1979 and 2017. During World War II, he was dismantled and sheltered from bomb damage in the Museum's basement, and in recent years he has even toured the United Kingdom to meet devoted dinosaur fans around the country.

Gryphaea

Fibonacci's law, like invisible ink,
has penned the ball of this stone shell;
the ridged years laid down
by a distant warm-sea-dream.

But if the Devil did have toes
they would be tipped with this
gnarled and stony claw,
prising itself out of the earth, feet first.

Halfway between the Devil's grin -
the glower of chalk teeth
amongst the folds of peat -
and the text books of my youth,

I have imagined this creature back to life,
setting it swimming between the trees
as I cross the path to home,
my thumb rubbing the idea of its back.

Wendy Pratt

Crinoid Fossils

Stars lie at your feet
some as small as a grain of sand
from when land was sea

Celia Warren

The Terror-Dragon's Thighbone

after the fall of the three kingdoms,
after the time of magician-emperors
who transformed to birds when they died.
in a time rich in bronze, jade and gold,

in our land between mountains and seas.
rice, peaches, silk, good things flourished.
we did not need oracle bones to tell
which way the wind was blowing,

spreading the fires of rebellion.
digging the field, my spade rang upon
a buried thing: hard but not stone,
long but not a rusted plough-tool,

caked in wet earth, a bone wide as
a young tree-trunk. I poured water upon it,
rubbed rough ivory with my sleeve,
prayed to the powerful emperor of

all creatures: oh terror-dragon, whose
stoneground bones cure sickness,
forgive me, poor yet blessed with children.
heaping yellow earth over the dragon's

thighbone, I bent once more to digging.
later that night by a lit moon, rolling
through cloud like a silver coin worn thin,
later I returned to claim it for my own.

Gita Ralleigh

She Finds Fossils

She sells seashells on the seashore –
Ammonite and belemnite
And much much more.
She's not a grand professor
Or a rich and famous man.
She's just a girl who earns her keep
And does the best she can.

She finds fossils on the cliff face.
She digs and dusts, makes her notes,
then presents her case.
There are scrapes, escapes and danger
Land slides, wild seas, wet sands
But with hammer, pick and basket
She does the best she can.

And . . . she discovers dinosaurs!
Plesiosaurus!
Ichthyosaurus too!
And lots and lots of coprolite – or . . . dinosaur poo!
She saw a Pterosaur – so she earned some fame,
Acknowledgement and some applause.
She began to make her name.

She found fame – but she deserved more.
Women like her were not expected to explore.
You can look up Mary Anning. Excavate, unearth her glory!
Dig away, make a display . . .
. . . and tell the world
　　　HER STORY.

Michaela Morgan

This oil painting of Mary Anning by an unknown artist was painted before 1842

Mary Anning (1799-1847)

Mary grew up in Lyme Regis, in Dorset. It is an area so rich in fossils that it's now known as the Jurassic Coast and her family sold specimens to supplement their meagre income. Like many girls at the time, Mary had no formal schooling but she taught herself geology and anatomy, and wasn't daunted by the landslide-prone cliffs. Among other discoveries, Mary found the first complete *Plesiosaurus* in 1823, and it flummoxed scientists. Many of them thought it was a fake before its authenticity was confirmed by a special meeting of the Geological Society in London which Mary – as a woman – wasn't permitted to attend. She also discovered the first pterosaur fossil found outside Germany, and was an early pioneer in the study of coprolites or dinosaur poo.

Mary's involvement in discoveries was often overlooked and ignored by the male scientific community, but she was instrumental in numerous important fossil finds, many of which can now be seen at the Natural History Museum. There are now several species named in her honour and in 2010 she was named by the Royal Society as one of the ten British women who have most influenced the history of science.

Remembering Mary

All night the sea has battered at the shore
and rain has run in torrents
'til the cliff has fallen, tumbled
in a dark and muddy heap.

Now the beach is rich with fossils
—sea lilies, feather stars, snakestones—
and fossil-hunters comb the sand,
walk with their eyes fixed downward,
scan the ground for creatures
dead a million years or more.

They are following
in Mary Anning's footsteps
who found the great fish-lizard
we call *Plesiosaur*.

The sea's mysterious –
iron grey and shunting shingle,
growling with the roll
of pebbles pounding in the tide.

This same long roar that fills us
as we beachcomb
this same long rolling roar
was sounding when Mary walked

below Black Ven.
It is the song that shapes the world
this echoing roar of dinosaurs –
the song of rocks and sea.

Jan Dean

Jurassic Coast

these stones sit still
until the sea strikes up the song
the shore-song shush of shingle
as salt says *dance with me*
then pebbles shimmy in the surf
spin in spume and tide

land and water in duet
rockfall   mudslip,
silt-fill   soil-shift,
mouths of rivers speak into the ocean
and the language of landslide
slurs earthbound fossils back towards the sea

Jan Dean

And as we followed dinosaurs

Whatever follows us
Will hunt for footprints in the lowlands,
And piece together fragments of our habits
From the internet.

A fossilised smartphone preserved behind glass
For the new young to traipse past on school trips,
Yawning.

Kae Tempest

Dinosaurs Walked Here

Dinosaurs walked here once.
Here, right here, on the site of this street,
they'd stamp along, and the slabs of their feet
were as wide as a car, crushing, crashing
a road through the reeds. Then, striding and splashing,
they'd thud in the mud of the deep green pool,
and they'd clomp in the swamp under new-forged skies
where now the cold grey concrete lies.
Or they'd stop, by the shop where we go for our snacks,
and with mouths gaping wide they'd commence their attacks.
Claw-jaw clash as they leapt on their prey,
who'd go desperately darting and dashing away.
But the beasts who were bigger would launch on their lunch
with a roar and a rip and lash-slash crunch.
Then perhaps where that cat's lying curled, they would sleep,
each of their bodies a truck-wide heap.
And see, on that building site, right over there,
their necks were cranes that rose in the air,
as tower block-tall they stood and sang
their ageless song, till the whole earth rang
with their voices, strong and clear and loud.
Lords of the land, they were, and proud
as they roamed their timeless realm. No more.
All there is now is the thunderous roar
of indifferent traffic, speeding on by.

The reeds are gone. The swamp is dry,
leaving only a puddle on paving stones.
Nothing remains. Not even bones.
But dinosaurs walked here,
once.

Elli Woollard

Dinosaur Sonnet

Dad sometimes calls the car a dinosaur,
but says that real dinosaurs have not been
around since grandpa was a kid, and laughs.
He is a real goof. If there are no
dinosaurs on the entire earth, then
why do people always talk about them?
In New York they have great dinosaur bones.
We do not know what skin they wore when they
were living. If we go extinct, how will
the scientists put our bones back together?
Octopi taste like chicken, but they are much
smarter than chickens. When the oceans grow
high, the octopi will study our
fossils by the wet ruins of Coney
Island. In the underwater towers
of Manhattan, side by side with our old
T. rex, they will imagine my favourite
foods, my bad dreams, the colour of my feet.

Camille Gagnier

Kronosaurus

See the bones hung from the roof
of the cool hall, how they look
like the ribs of a boat. The hull
and keel, the long body tapered

to a point. A million years have
stripped it to its struts. Once,
a dip in the ocean might have brought
you face to face – imagine that!

Thirty feet of brute strength
and teeth, faster than a shark,
snap snap snapping at your heels
in dark water. Doesn't that give you pause

for thought? It's quite enough to make me
glad of giant squid, and jellyfish, and even
Jaws. I'd rather share the sea with *them*
than a single hungry pliosaur . . .

Cheryl Pearson

Apatosaurus Rap

Some say I'm square . . . But that's just my snout.

I'm one of the funkiest lizards about.

I weigh 20 tons, which is plenty to haul,

But me? I don't care! (Well, my brain is quite small.)

I'd weigh a lot more, but I've air in my bones

and I live on a diet of algae and stones.

My talented tail has a delicate tip –

I like nothing more than to give it a whip.

It's crazily long, so you'd better make room

and then cover your ears for the thunderous

B O o O o o O o o o O o o o o O o M .

Scientists have used computer simulation to calculate that the VERY long tail of the Apatosaurus would have reached 200 decibels, which means it would have BROKEN THE SOUND BARRIER with every whip!

It was one of the biggest animals to have ever roamed the Earth, even though it only ate greens. (Well, it did eat a lot – about the weight of two pianos a day.)

Laura Mucha

Dear Stegosaurus

Bus-sized and gentle, you are master of peace,
diplomacy, berries, grass, perseverance, pace.

Your warm, rough belly sags with majesty over ferns,
cycads and dust. Your spikes are dull and magnificent,

a row of abandoned kites, rusted by a tough winter,
in a tree stripped of guts. You're not a fighter, though

you will fight. It's hard to just stay out of trouble
when everyone else is looking for it, I know. Tinted red

and armoured, I think I couldn't know more beauty
if I travelled the earth ten thousand times.

The perfections of your tiny head trounce a sunset,
your mouth holds more wonder than a sky full of stars.

Rebecca Perry

The most complete *Stegosaurus* skeleton ever discovered can be seen at the
Museum and she is affectionately known as 'Sophie'. Sophie lived in modern
day Wyoming during the Jurassic Period, around 150 million years ago, and
was a herbivore. She had bony plates along her back and a viciously spiked tail
to defend herself from predators and, although she would have been around
nine metres long, her brain was only the size of a plum.

Velociraptors

velociraptors were not voluptuous
some say they climbed trees, mostly coniferous

their name is said to mean swift seizer,
nifty plunderer, lightning geezer

they roamed this planet in times cretaceous
to little reptiles they were vexatious

with a sickle-shaped claw on the second toe
the prey was hooked: nowhere to go

the size of a small child, ideal for show-and-tell
note the strange mark where your teacher fell

Rob Walton

The King of All the Dinosaurs

With taloned feet and razor claws,
Leathery scales, monstrous jaws . . .
The king of all the dinosaurs
Tyrannosaurus rex.

With sabre teeth no one ignores,
It rants and raves and royally roars . . .
The king of all the dinosaurs
Tyrannosaurus rex.

The largest of the carnivores,
It stomps and chomps on forest floors . . .
The king of all the dinosaurs
Tyrannosaurus rex.

Charges forwards, waging wars,
Gouges, gorges, gashes, gores . . .
The king of all the dinosaurs
Tyrannosaurus rex.

With taloned feet and razor claws,
Leathery scales, monstrous jaws,
Sabre teeth no one ignores,
It rants and raves and royally roars . . .
The king of all the dinosaurs
Tyrannosaurus rex.

Paul Cookson

Part of the first *Tyrannosaurus rex* skeleton ever to be discovered is on display at the Museum. But if you like a little more action, one of the Museum's most loved – and feared – exhibits is the animatronic *T. rex* that thrashes its tail and roars at thrilled visitors. At four metres high, it's around three-quarters the size that the real dinosaur would have been – but every bit as imposing!

This Is How We Walked

This is how we walked, all those years ago — those hundreds, thousands and millions of years that we spent, pressing ourselves to the mud. Into sand and seabed, forest floor and mountain side. We ran on two or sometimes four legs, swam or flew. Paddled, dabbled, were

experimental. Were a practise run. Were evolution. Some of us were fast, some of us slow. No matter – we almost mostly got there in the end. Plod or gallop, go lightly or galumph, we lived for a while as giants, grand as pianos, big as buses, broad as vans.

Measuring our steps can tell you our speed or weight but not the colour of the moon above as we surrendered ourselves to the silt. Some secrets we have kept.

You have learned the size of
our throats but not the
sound of our songs.

Jane Burn

The Night Flight of the Pterodactyl

As I wait for the right current of air
a moonbeam glistens on my claw.

I take off from the highest mountain –
not without grace,
not without speed,
and with a spine of pride
which tingles to my gleaming teeth –
I'm the largest creature to fly.

Gliding over the lake I make
a black shadow with my shape,
warm blood pumps through my jaw.

I swoop on a sleeping frog,
look up at the swarming stars,
then end his dream with a snap.

Chrissie Gittins

This beautiful illustration of the Great Horned Owl comes from John James Audubon's famous Birds of America

'All nature listens silent to him' – Birds

Would you believe that the friendly robin is a distant descendant of *Tyrannosaurus rex?* In the twentieth century it was discovered that some dinosaurs had feathers and many bird-like qualities. Palaeontologists now believe that the gradual evolution from two-legged dinosaurs that ran on the ground to small, winged birds that could fly began around 160 million years ago. Birds now live on every continent and are astonishingly diverse. They are united by having feathers, a beak and a fused collarbone also known as the wishbone.

The Natural History Museum's world-class bird collections include nearly a million pickled, pressed, dried, skinned and mounted specimens covering around 95% of all known bird species, an impressive collection of nests, and over a million individual eggs. Visitors can marvel at the impressive wingspan of a soaring albatross and the glamorous plumage of the golden pheasant, as well as viewing some of John James Audubon's famous paintings from his giant masterpiece *The Birds of America*.

Listening to

Brrrrrrrrrrreeeeeeeeep

Iiiip iiiiip iiiiip

Raarp rarrp rarrp rarrp

Deecha deecha deecha

Ssshhh-chhh-chhh-ssshhh-chhh-chhh

Ooooweepooweepooweep

Nndurrrrrr nndurrrrrr

Gyaaaaayk gyaaaaayk

1) Wren (brrrrrrrrrrreeeeeeeeep), 2) Long-tailed tit (liiip iiiiip iiiiip), 3) Raven (raarp rarrp rarrp rarrp), 4) Great tit (deecha deecha deecha), 5) Wren (ssshhh-chhh-chhh-ssshhh-chhh-chhh), 6) Willow warbler (ooooweepooweepooweep), 7) Wood pigeon (nndurrrrrr nndurrrrrr), 8) Herring gull (gyaaaaayk gyaaaaayk).

Laura Mucha

Proud Songsters

The thrushes sing as the sun is going,
And the finches whistle in ones and pairs,
And as it gets dark loud nightingales
     In bushes
Pipe, as they can when April wears,
  As if all Time were theirs.

These are brand-new birds of twelve-months' growing,
Which a year ago, or less than twain,
No finches were, nor nightingales,
     Nor thrushes,
But only particles of grain,
  And earth, and air, and rain.

Thomas Hardy

The Peace of Wild Things

When despair for the world grows in me
and I wake in the night at the least sound
in fear of what my life and children's lives may be,
I go and lie down where the wood drake
rests in his beauty on the water, and the great heron feeds.
I come into the peace of wild things
who do not tax their lives with forethought
of grief. I come into the presence of still water.
And I feel above me the day-blind stars
waiting with their light. For a time
I rest in the grace of the world, and am free.

Wendell Berry

Kingfisher

Kingfisher: the colour-giver, fire-bringer, flame-flicker,
    river's quiver.
Ink-black bill, orange throat, and a quick blue
    back-gleaming feather-stream.
Neat and still it sits on the snag of a stick, until with . . .
Gold-flare, wing-fan, whipcrack the kingfisher –
    zingfisher, singfisher! –
Flashes down too fast to follow, quick and quicker
    carves its hollow
In the water, slings its arrow superswift to swallow
Stickleback or shrimp or minnow.
Halcyon is its other name – also ripple-calmer,
    water-nester,
Evening angler, weather-teller, rainbringer and
Rainbow bird – that sets the stream alight with burn
    and glitter!

Robert Macfarlane

Swan and Shadow

<pre>
                    Dusk
                Above the
        water   hang   the
                    loud
                    flies
                    Here
                    O so
                    gray
                    then
                What   A pale signal will appear
                When   Soon before its shadow fades
                Where   Here in this pool of opened eye
                In us   No Upon us As at the very edges
            of where we take shape in the dark air
            this object bares its image awakening
                ripples of recognition that will
                    brush darkness up into light
even after this bird this hour both drift by atop the perfect sad instant now
                    already passing out of sight
                    toward yet-untroubled reflection
            this image bears its object darkening
            into memorial shades Scattered bits of
            light   No of water Or something across
            water   Breaking up No Being regathered
            soon   Yet by then a swan will have
                gone   Yes out of mind into what
                    vast
                    pale
                    hush
                    of a
                    place
                    past
        sudden   dark   as
            if   a swan
                    sang
</pre>

John Hollander

Grey Geese

All night they flew over in skeins.
I heard their wrangling far away
Went out once to look for them, long
     after midnight.
Saw them silvered by the moonlight, like waves,
Flagging south, jagged and tired,
Across the sleeping farms and the autumn rivers
To the late fields of autumn.

Even in a city I have heard them
Their noise like the rusty wheel of a bicycle;
I have looked up from among the drum of engines
To find them in the sky
A broken arrowhead turning south
Heading for home.

The Iceland summer, the long light
Has run like rivers through their wings,
Strengthened the sinews of their flight
Over the whole ocean, till at last they circle,
Straggle down on the chosen runway of
     their field.

They come back
To the same place, the same day, without fail;
Precision instruments, a compass
Somewhere deep in their souls.

Kenneth C. Steven

Swallowed

When humans didn't know any better,
all the swallows flew to the moon each autumn
and returned to planet earth in spring.

And since the moon has no stoneflies, sawflies,
mayflies, damselflies, the swallows adapted, got fat
on mooncrumbs and double cream.

And as there wasn't much of an atmosphere,
no air up there for sound to travel in, the swallows fell
quite silent for a full six months

or so they told us each April, by then bursting
to spill a backlog of chatter. Hundreds of years
it took us. Hundreds – to catch up, cotton on, *capeesh*

that the other side of the world exists
and that's where the birds go to winter.
Nowadays they send us postcards from Maputo,

Kruger, Bulawayo, Drakensberg, The Cape.
Or they WhatsApp us snaps of a sunset, desert, beach
sometimes adding in (LOL) a splash of cream.

Shauna Darling Robertson

Blackbird

The blackbird is
a common bird,
a sleek shadow-feathered
boy, who sings out from a
golden bill, with little gaps
for joy. He lifts his voice when
rain has passed and washed the
garden clean, and drizzles notes
of loveliness upon the damp, lush
green. A summer sound, like
soaring lark, but clear and
true and strong, he whistles and
the world becomes
blackbird
blue sky
Song!

Liz Brownlee

The Lark's Song

Thou hearest the Nightingale begin the Song of
    Spring;
The lark sitting upon his earthy bed, just as the morn
Appears, listens silent, then springing from the waving
    Corn-field, loud
He leads the Choir of Day-trill, trill, trill, trill,
Mounting upon the wing of light into the Great
    Expanse,
Re-echoing against the lovely blue and shining
    heavenly Shell,
His little throat labours with inspiration, every feather
On throat and breast and wings vibrates with the
    effluence Divine.
All nature listens silent to him, and the awful Sun
Stands still upon the Mountain looking on this little
    Bird
With eyes of soft humility and wonder, love, and awe.

William Blake

Little Trotty Wagtail

Little trotty wagtail, he went in the rain,
And tittering, tottering sideways he ne'er got straight again.
He stooped to get a worm, and look'd up to catch a fly,
And then he flew away ere his feathers they were dry.

Little trotty wagtail, he waddled in the mud,
And left his little footmarks, trample where he would.
He waddled in the water-pudge, and waggle went his tail,
And he chirrupt up his wings to dry upon the garden rail.

Little trotty wagtail, you nimble all about,
And in the dimpling water-pudge you waddle in and out;
Your home is nigh at hand, and in the warm pigsty,
So, little Master Wagtail, I'll bid you a goodbye.

John Clare

Humming-bird

I can imagine, in some otherworld
Primeval-dumb, far back
In that most awful stillness, that only gasped and hummed,
Humming-birds raced down the avenues.

Before anything had a soul,
While life was a heave of Matter, half inanimate,
This little bit chipped off in brilliance
And went whizzing through the slow, vast, succulent stems.

I believe there were no flowers then,
In the world where the humming-bird flashed ahead of creation.
I believe he pierced the slow vegetable veins with his long beak.

Probably he was big
As mosses, and little lizards, they say, were once big.
Probably he was a jabbing, terrifying monster.

We look at him through the wrong end of the long telescope of Time,
Luckily for us.

D. H. Lawrence

One of the Museum's most intriguing treasures is a Victorian cabinet filled with more than a hundred stuffed humming-bird specimens from South America. Even though the jewel tones of their plumage have faded over time, it's still strikingly beautiful. Humming-birds are the only birds that can fly backwards, and the very smallest weigh no more than a paperclip.

Green Bee-eater

More precious than all
the gems of Jaipur –

the green bee-eater.

If you see one singing
tree-tree-tree

with his space-black bill
and rufous cap,

his robes
all shades of emerald

like treetops glimpsed
from a plane,

his blue cheeks,
black eye-mask

and the delicate tail streamer
like a plume of smoke –

you might dream
of the forests

that once clothed
our flying planet.

And perhaps his singing
is a spell

to call our forests back –

tree
    by *tree*
        by *tree.*

Pascale Petit

Indian Paradise Flycatcher

your tail two comets
  of ice crystals
    your face a night-
      blue sheen

      as if dipped
    in starlight
   your wings snowdrifts
from a past climate

you descend
  in a heat haze
    and when you dip
      into a pool

      you're a pen
   sky-writing
  on a mirror
a flick of flakes

melting
  a jet's contrails
    telling us
      about a sun fuelled

by frost
Too fast for my eye
your tail streamers
weave an alphabet

to cool the earth
you dinosaur-relic
little white flag
from the Holocene

Pascale Petit

Parrots

'Now I go to my dinner,
For all day I've been a-
way at the West End,
Painting the best end
Of some vast Parrots
As red as new carrots,—
(They are at the museum,—
When you come you shall see 'em,—)
I do the head and neck first;
—And ever since breakfast,
I've had one bun merely!
So—yours quite sincerely.'

Edward Lear

The Cockatiel, by Edward Lear

Edward Lear (1812-1888)

Although now remembered for his humorous verses including 'The Owl and The Pussy-cat', Edward Lear was also a talented artist — in fact, he even gave Queen Victoria drawing lessons. Aged only nineteen, he produced a series of beautiful illustrations of parrots and — unlike most artists of the day, who worked from stuffed specimens — he spent hours at the London Zoological Gardens studying and even measuring living birds. Sometimes he included cheeky portraits of the gawking public in the background of his sketches.

Parrots

parrots
with vermilion bands and beak
green-iris camouflaging
are acrobats
swinging on trapezes of green gum leaves
tips

they carry their very own safety net
their green-yellow tail feathers
which spray out like palm fronds
parachuting

Neil Paech

Arctic Tern

Love has to take us unawares
for none of us would pay love's price if we knew it.
For who will pay to be destroyed?
The destruction is so certain,
so evident.

Much harder to chart,
less evident,
is love's second life,
a tern's egg,
revealed and hidden
in a nest of stones
on a stony shore.

What seems a stone
is no stone.
This vulnerable pulse
which could be held in the palm of a hand
may survive
to voyage the world's warm and frozen oceans,
its tapered wings,
the beat of its small heart,
a span between arctic poles.

Moya Cannon

The Eagle

He clasps the crag with crooked hands;
Close to the sun in lonely lands,
Ringed with the azure world, he stands.

The wrinkled sea beneath him crawls;
He watches from his mountain walls,
And like a thunderbolt he falls.

Alfred, Lord Tennyson

Hawk Roosting

I sit in the top of the wood, my eyes closed.
Inaction, no falsifying dream
Between my hooked head and hooked feet:
Or in sleep rehearse perfect kills and eat.

The convenience of the high trees!
The air's buoyancy and the sun's ray
Are of advantage to me;
And the earth's face upward for my inspection.

My feet are locked upon the rough bark.
It took the whole of Creation
To produce my foot, my each feather:
Now I hold Creation in my foot

Or fly up, and revolve it all slowly –
I kill where I please because it is all mine.
There is no sophistry in my body:
My manners are tearing off heads –

The allotment of death.
For the one path of my flight is direct
Through the bones of the living.
No arguments assert my right:

The sun is behind me.
Nothing has changed since I began.
My eye has permitted no change.
I am going to keep things like this.

Ted Hughes

Owl Poem

Every flower is blue at night. Every field
of wheat. Navy sleeves the wood.

Two eyes marry the dark on a moonless branch.
Ring to ring, bright gold.

Their hoots are gently bowled. They gather
mice bones, moss.

What settles a grief? The owl knows. Blood
for a blue mood,

a hunger. See how they float. White and silent.
Snow falling on water.

Cheryl Pearson

Dear Egg

Dear Egg,
you'll have to do this
one day: stand
in the ice-burst-
bone-chill winds
of the Antarctic as
they blow-blast-blitz
your feathers, feet tightly
together to shield a little
Emperor-in-the-making   from
The blizzard's burn. Or maybe
it will be you who swims for
miles below the ice, searching
for food for your love-snuggled
egg back on shore. When you
do, when the bitter cold bites
harder than a hungry elephant
seal, remember this: you
//// are loved. From
//   Father

Laura Mucha

The Dodo

The Dodo used to walk
around,
And take the sun and air.
The sun yet warms his
native ground –
The Dodo is not there!

The voice which used to
squawk and squeak
Is now for ever dumb –
Yet may you see his bones
and beak
All in the Mu-se-um.

Hilaire Belloc

The Dodo - this model is based on modern interpretations which suggest a slimmer body than previous thought

The dodo lived on the island of Mauritius, off Africa's east coast. It couldn't fly, but it survived on fruit and nuts it scavenged on the ground – until humans arrived on its island home at the start of the seventeenth century. As well as the dodos being hunted for food, the rats, cats and pigs brought by the Dutch settlers feasted on the eggs in their ground-level nests, and by the end of the century the poor dodo was extinct. The demise of the species had been so rapid that some scientists later thought the dodo had been invented by sailors spinning tall tales, and there is much we still don't know about them. The Museum's dodo skeleton is actually a composite formed from several different birds, since so few complete or almost complete dodo skeletons survive.

Plate XXVI, The Green Fly

From The Aurelian: or, Natural History of Insects; Namely Moths and Butterflies together with the plants on which they fed. by Moses Harris, Secretary to the Aurelian Society, 1766.

'Hurt no Living Thing' – Creepy Crawlies

Insects make up more than 50% of known species on earth and are the largest and most diverse group of living animals, having a tremendous impact on our planet as everything from pest to pollinator. The Museum houses around thirty-seven million insect specimens. Passionate private collectors have been sending samples to the Museum since it opened, and many of them are stored in the original – now antique – cigarette boxes and newspapers in which they arrived. Scientists can learn much from the study of insects, known as entomology, because changes in their populations can herald environmental trends that will affect our whole world.

The Creepy Crawlies gallery includes a life-sized model of a termite mound and one of the Museum's few live exhibits: a busy colony of leaf-cutter ants. A model house showing where mites, wasps and fleas might be found in our own homes certainly provides some food for thought! Among the Museum's most curious holdings are a set of outfits including wedding costumes for fleas made by Mexican nuns and an intricate wasp's nest in a bowler hat, both held at the Museum's sister branch at Tring in Hertfordshire.

Have you ever

held any amber? A solid block of honey,
clear and gold, old as time? If you're lucky,
you will find there's a bug stuck inside –
when that thick 'n sticky syrup would
have oozed then dried. And it's all we'll
ever see of that sky-scraper, forest-maker
ghost of a tree. Like a poem, built to last:
it's a gift from the past, in your hand a
small reminder, yellow wonder,
precious chunk of ancient amber.

James Carter

Of Bees

from Georgics, Book IV

Of all the race of animals, alone,
The bees have common cities of their own;
And, common sons, beneath one law they live,
And with one common stock their traffic drive.
Each has a certain home, a sev'ral stall;
All is the State's, the State provides for all.
Mindful of coming cold, they share the pain,
And hoard, for winter's use, the summer's gain.
Some o'er the public magazines preside,
And some are sent new forage to provide;
These drudge in fields abroad, and those at home
Lay deep foundations for the labor'd comb,
With dew, narcissus leaves, and clammy gum.
To pitch the waxen flooring some contrive;
Some nurse the future nation of the hive;
Sweet honey some condense; some purge the grout;
The rest, in cells apart, the liquid nectar shut:
All, with united force, combine to drive
The lazy drones from the laborious hive;
With envy stung, they view each other's deeds;
With diligence the fragrant work proceeds.

Virgil

Virgil's Bees

Bless air's gift of sweetness, honey
from the bees, inspired by clover,
marigold, eucalyptus, thyme,
the hundred perfumes of the wind.
Bless the beekeeper

            who chooses for her hives
a site near water, violet beds, no yew,
no echo. Let the light lilt, leak, green
or gold, pigment for queens,
and joy be inexplicable but *there*
in harmony of willowherb and stream,
of summer heat and breeze,
                    each bee's body
at its brilliant flower, lover-stunned,
strumming on fragrance, smitten.

                  For this,
let gardens grow, where beelines end,
sighing in roses, saffron blooms, buddleia;
where bees pray on their knees, sing, praise
in pear trees, plum trees; bees
are the batteries of orchards, gardens, guard them.

Carol Ann Duffy

Fireflies in the Garden

Here come real stars to fill the upper skies,
And here on earth come emulating flies,
That though they never equal stars in size,
(And they were never really stars at heart)
Achieve at times a very star-like start.
Only, of course, they can't sustain the part.

Robert Frost

Mayfly May

Mayfly May, may only fly for a day,
but she has the most delicate   wings –
lacy, transparent, exquisite, fine,
drawn   with   the   thinnest   black   line.

Mayfly May has no need of a mouth,
she has no need of food –
she   must   find   a   mate   before   the   afternoon   gets   late,
then lay her eggs on the water.

Her eggs drift down to   the   river's   ground
where they hatch into nymphs by the thousand.
They   shed   their   skin   over   twenty times,
two years later they rise   in the   water.

May's mayflies flit in the bright sunlight
with the myriads flicking   across   woodland.
May may have flown for only one day –
but millions   of   mayfly   will   follow.

Chrissie Gittins

The Caterpillar

Brown and furry
Caterpillar in a hurry,
Take your walk
To the shady leaf, or stalk,
Or what not,
Which may be the chosen spot.
No toad to spy you,
Hovering bird of prey pass by you;
Spin and die,
To live again a butterfly.

Christina Rossetti

The Dream of the Cabbage Caterpillars

There was no magic spell:
all of us, sleeping,
dreamed the same dream – a dream
that's ours for the keeping

In sunbeam or dripping rain,
sister by brother
we once roamed with glee
the leaves that our mother

laid us and left us on,
browsing our fill
of green cabbage, fresh cabbage,
thick cabbage, until

in the hammocks we hung
from the garden wall
came sleep, and the dream
that changed us all –

we had left our soft bodies,
the munching, the crawling,
to skim through the clear air
like white petals falling!

Just so, so we woke –
so to skip high as towers,
and dip now to sweet fuel
from trembling bright flowers.

Libby Houston

The Painted Lady

The Painted Lady is a small African
butterfly, gayly toned orchid or peach
that seems as tremulous and delicately sheer
as the objects I treasure, yet, this cosmopolitan
can cross the sea at the icy time of the year
in the trail of the big boats, to France.
Mischance is as wide and somber grey as the lake here
in Chicago. Is there strength enough in my huge
peach paper rose, or lavender sea-laced fan?

Margaret Danner

Butterfly

On wings flake-fragile,
petal-frail, you somehow sail,
mile after long mile.

Kate Williams

Plate XXI, The Unicorn
From The Aurelian: or, Natural History of Insects; Namely
Moths and Butterflies together with the plants on which they
fed, by Moses Harris, Secretary to the Aurelian Society, 1766.

145

Life-cycle of the Moth

Each word or phrase is the name of an actual moth.

Peach-blossom, muslin. Sallow kitten,
Gipsy.

Dark tussock, satin carpet.
Wood-leopard, scarlet tiger!

Great prominent,
Iron prominent –
Dark crimson underwing.

Emperor, white ermine,
Large emerald.

December. Frosted green.
Lackey, red-necked footman.
Drinker.
Scarce silver.

Old lady,
Figure of eighty,
Death's head,
Vapourer.

Ghost swift.

Elma Mitchell

Beast

Doyen of the dead night. Silent goth.
Bullet-bodied babe of light-lured wrath.
Spell-born grub-spawn from a witchcraft broth.

Papery wings of powdery cloth
Dyed the dark hues of the cauldron's froth.
Shadow of a butterfly. Fluttering moth.

Nick Toczek

A Noiseless, Patient Spider

A noiseless patient spider,
I mark'd where on a little promontory it stood isolated,
Mark'd how to explore the vacant vast surrounding,
It launched forth filament, filament, filament, out of itself,
Ever unreeling them, ever tirelessly speeding them.

And you O my soul where you stand,
Surrounded, detached, in measureless oceans of space,
Ceaselessly musing, venturing, throwing, seeking the spheres to connect them,
Till the bridge you will need be form'd, till the ductile anchor hold,
Till the gossamer thread you fling catch somewhere, O my soul.

Walt Whitman

Snail Spell

Snail you
prosper slippery
in rain's looking glass
dropping crystal runes
on rings of moss

skimming four pebble
toad bronze eyes
across leaf lakes
of autumn fire

till dusk

then pick
at the moon
scraps of sky
taste the earth gold
on breath of night

over flower mountain
dank, strawberry mist
eat darkness slowly
until it goes.

Sue Hardy Dawson

A Snail's Advice to His Son
after Gervase Phinn

Always keep your shell clean, son.
It shows the world you care.
Hold your antennae straight and proud
and pointing in the air.

Trail your slime in crisp, clean lines
in parallel to walls,
stick to grass where dogs are banned
(and games involving balls).

If you must steal mankind's veg
wait till they're not around.
Steer well clear of allotments ('least
until the sun's gone down).

Although you may not have one, son,
be sure to chance your arm.
Confronted by a gang of slugs,
let your response be calm.

Keep your head in times of stress
(inside your shell, if poss).
When I am gone, just carry on.
Smile, despite your loss.

Keep that sense of patience,
never let your stride be rushed;
and don't take life too seriously, son,
for few survive uncrushed.

Jamie McGarry

Cockroach

Scuttle-bug,
shadow-foot,
bringer of night;
sky without stars,
obsidian-light;
shiny as coal,
new-mined and still bright;
smooth as new carbon,
dark and untyped.

Judith Nicholls

Sketch

Belly-up woodlouse on this desk:
lifeboat-like, all paddles raised,
drifting deeper into calmer waters.

A. F. Harrold

On the Grasshopper and the Cricket

The poetry of earth is never dead:
    When all the birds are faint with the hot sun,
    And hide in cooling trees, a voice will run
From hedge to hedge about the new-mown mead;
That is the Grasshopper's – he takes the lead
    In summer luxury, – he has never done
    With his delights; for when tired out with fun
He rests at ease beneath some pleasant weed.

The poetry of earth is ceasing never:
    On a lone winter evening, when the frost
    Has wrought a silence, from the stove there shrills
The Cricket's song, in warmth increasing ever,
    And seems to one in drowsiness half lost,
    The Grasshopper's among some grassy hills.

John Keats

The Grasshopper

Origami made him from a leaf
folded into minute symmetries

of eye and wing, long hind legs
fitted for leaping and music-making.

One day he elbowed his way up
out of the mire to sing of love

and of his perfectly broken heart –
O, such meagre tinder for a fire!

Katharine Towers

The Ants

What wonder strikes the curious, while he views
The black ant's city, by a rotten tree,
Or woodland bank! In ignorance we muse:
Pausing, annoy'd, – we know not what we see,
Such government and thought there seem to be;
Some looking on, and urging some to toil,
Dragging their loads of bent-stalks slavishly:
And what's more wonderful, when big loads foil
One ant or two to carry, quickly then
A swarm flock round to help their fellow-men.
Surely they speak a language whisperingly,
Too fine for us to hear; and sure their ways
Prove they have kings and laws, and that they be
Deformed remnants of the Fairy-days.

John Clare

Hurt No Living Thing

Hurt no living thing,
Ladybird nor butterfly,
Nor moth with dusty wing,
Nor cricket chirping cheerily,
Nor grasshopper, so light of leap,
Nor dancing gnat,
Nor beetle fat,
Nor harmless worms that creep.

Christina Rossetti

A beautiful illustration of mammals from Dr Hermann
Burmeister's Atlas (1835)

'How heavy is a whale's dream?' – Mammals

Nobody forgets their first visit to the Mammals gallery in which visitors to the Museum can come face to face with a throng of animals of all shapes and sizes from all corners of the world. From the hippo to the tiny pygmy shrew, and from a double-tusked narwhal to the extinct sabre-toothed cat, models, skeletons, interactive displays and taxidermy bring the animal kingdom to vivid life.

The Museum has one of the largest collections of taxidermy – or stuffed animal specimens – in the world although less than half of it is on display at any time.

Tenants of Paradise

from Paradise Lost, IV

About them frisking played
All beasts of the earth, since wild, and of all chase
In wood or wilderness, forest or den;
Sporting the lion ramped, and in his paw
Dandled the kid; bears, tigers, ounces, pards,
Gamboled before them, the unwieldy elephant
To make them mirth used all his might, and wreathed
His lithe proboscis; close the serpent sly
Insinuating, wove with Gordian twine
His braided train, and of his fatal guile
Gave proof unheeded; others on the grass
Couched, and now filled with pasture gazing sat,
Or bedward ruminating . . .

John Milton

The Natural History Museum

They are glassed and boxed like childhood,
the dead creatures in their pastoral
dance: the grinning fox and pouting squirrel,
the ferrets in their stiff quadrille. Parents nod
and watch their children watch the bloodshed
always about to happen: the wee mouse
cower, the wildcat locked in a pointless
leap. It was Bosch, I think, who painted
the Cat padding into Eden with a small beast
limp in her mouth. A child smiles. Her father
aims a camera. He shoots, and does not ask
what the half-silvered hare asserts,
stopped on the cusp of change, forever
almost escaping, kicking his heels at the dark.

Kate Clanchy

Badgers

Badgers come creeping from dark under ground,
Badgers scratch hard with a bristly sound,
Badgers go nosing around.

Badgers have whiskers and black and white faces,
Badger cubs scramble and scrap and run races,
Badgers like overgrown places.

Badgers don't jump when a vixen screams,
Badgers drink quietly from moonshiny streams,
Badgers dig holes in our dreams.

Badgers are working while you and I sleep,
Pushing their tunnels down twisting and steep,
Badgers have secrets to keep.

Richard Edwards

The Fox

A hundred yards from the peak, while the bells
Of the churches on the slopes called to prayer
And the unspent sun of marvellous July
Called to the mountain, – it was then,
On unfelt feet and with silent stride,
He paced his rare wonders before us.
We did not move, we did not breathe,
A moment paralysed; like a trinity in stone
We stood, while in untroubled midstep
He paused in surprise, and above
His single hesitant step the two steady flames
Of his eyes held us.
Then, without haste or fear,
He slipped his russet coat over the ridge;
It happened, it ended, like a shooting star.

Robert Williams Parry
translated from the Welsh by Barry Tobin

The Fawn

There it was I saw what I shall never forget
And never retrieve.
Monstrous and beautiful to human eyes, hard to believe,
He lay, yet there he lay,
Asleep on the moss, his head on his polished cleft small ebony hooves,
The child of the doe, the dappled child of the deer.

Surely his mother had never said, 'Lie here
Till I return,' so spotty and plain to see
On the green moss lay he.
His eyes had opened; he considered me.

I would have given more than I care to say
To thrifty ears, might I have had him for my friend
One moment only of that forest day:

Might I have had the acceptance, not the love
Of those clear eyes;
Might I have been for him in the bough above
Or the root beneath his forest bed,
A part of the forest, seen without surprise.

Was it alarm, or was it the wind of my fear lest he depart
That jerked him to his jointy knees,
And sent him crashing off, leaping and stumbling
On his new legs, between the stems of the white trees?

Edna St Vincent Millay

The Sloth

In moving-slow he has no Peer.
You ask him something in his ear;
He thinks about it for a Year;

And, then, before he says a Word
There, upside down (unlike a Bird)
He will assume that you have Heard—

A most Ex-as-per-at-ing Lug.
But should you call his manner Smug,
He'll sigh and give his Branch a Hug;

Then off again to Sleep he goes,
Still swaying gently by his Toes,
And you just *know* he knows he knows.

Theodore Roethke

A popular attraction at the Museum is the replica ground sloth skeleton. *Megatherium* – which means 'great beast' – was a huge shaggy-furred, long-clawed sloth found in South America from 400,000 to 8,000 years ago. It would have stood up to 3.5 metres high on its hind legs and weighed as much as a modern bull elephant, and Charles Darwin was among the scientists who gathered fossil evidence of this impressive animal.

Monkey

I am
swing-on-a-tail,
up with the sun
fast as white lightning
slits skies at noon.
Now under palms,
now over fern;
dawn-creeper, branch-leaper,
dive, twist and turn.
Face-in-the-forest,
chasing the moon;
tree-lover, sky-brother,
dew-dancing one.

Judith Nicholls

Gorillas

Moonlight upon the mountains
And the gentle Gorillas awake

They lumber along through the forest
To sit by the side of the lake

And there in the silvery water
They dangle their ticklish toes

And what the Gorillas are thinking
Nobody nobody knows

Adrian Mitchell

Despite his impressive stature and occasional temper, Guy the gorilla – a much-loved resident at London Zoo during his lifetime – was a big softy who was so scared of the fireworks when he arrived on 5th November 1947 that a keeper slept over with him. Guy had been observed scooping up the no doubt rather alarmed sparrows that found themselves in his enclosure and examining them before carefully letting them go. After his death during a dental operation in 1978, it took the Museum's head taxidermist nearly nine months to preserve his splendour.

Elephant Eternity

Elephants walking under juicy-leaf trees
Walking with their children under juicy-leaf trees
Elephants elephants walking like time

Elephants bathing in the foam-floody river
Fountaining their children in the mothery river
Elephants elephants bathing like happiness

    Strong and gentle elephants
    Standing on the earth
    Strong and gentle elephants
    Like peace

Time is walking under elephant trees
Happiness is bathing in the elephant river
Strong gentle peace is shining
All over the elephant earth

Adrian Mitchell

The Elephant

When people bear this beast to mind,
They marvel more and more
At such a LITTLE tail behind,
So LARGE a trunk before.

Hilaire Belloc

Lion

The lion, ruler over all the beasts,
Triumphant moves upon the grassy plain
With sun like gold upon his tawny brow
And dew like silver on his shaggy mane.

Into himself he draws the rolling thunder,
Beneath his flinty paw great boulders quake;
He will dispatch the mouse to burrow under,
The little deer to shiver in the brake.

He sets the fierce whip of each serpent lashing,
The tall giraffe brings humbly to his knees,
Awakes the sloth, and sends the wild boar crashing,
Wide-eyed monkeys chittering, through the trees.

He gazes down into the quiet river,
Parting the green bulrushes to behold
A sunflower-crown of amethyst and silver,
A royal coat of brushed and beaten gold.

William Jay Smith

The Museum holds the skull of a Barbary lion which lived in the Royal Menagerie, established at the Tower of London in the thirteenth century to house the monarch's collection of exotic animals. The skull was excavated from the Tower's moat, where the skeleton had been preserved since medieval times. Among the other animals to grace the Menagerie between the 1200s and 1835 were jackals, an elephant and even a polar bear who hunted for fish in the Thames. When the remaining animals were re-housed in the nineteenth century, they became the first inhabitants of London Zoo.

Otter

Otter enters river without falter – what a
    supple slider out of holt and into water!

This shape-shifter's a sheer breath-taker, a
    sure heart-stopper – but you'll only ever spot
    a shadow-flutter, bubble-skein, and never
    (almost never) actual otter.

This swift swimmer's a silver-miner – with
    trout its ore it bores each black pool deep
    and deeper, delves up-current steep and
    steeper, turns the water inside-out, then
    inside-outer.

Ever dreamed of being otter? That
    utter underwater thunderbolter, that
    shimmering twister?

Run to the riverbank, otter-dreamer, slip
    your skin and change your matter, pour
    your outer being into otter – and enter
    now as otter without falter into water.

Robert Macfarlane

The Platypus

My child, the Duck-billed Platypus
A sad example sets for us:
From him we learn how Indecision
Of character provokes Derision.
This vacillating Thing, you see,
Could not decide which he would be,
Fish, Flesh or Fowl, and chose all three.
The scientists were sorely vexed
To classify him; so perplexed
Their brains, that they, with Rage at bay,
Called him a horrid name one day,—
A name that baffles, frights and shocks us,
Ornithorhynchus Paradoxus.

Oliver Herford

The Duck-billed Platypus, painted by Ferdinand Lucas Bauer on an expedition to Australia 1801-1803

So extraordinary a beast is the duck-billed platypus that when the Museum's specimen arrived in Europe from Australia in 1798, many scientists were convinced it was a fake. There had been 'mythical' beasts constructed before, including a fish-tailed monkey, but this strange bird-billed furry beast turned out to be genuine. These most primitive of warm-blooded animals are one of only a small handful that lay eggs, and they can also – very unusually for mammals – produce venom.

Seal Lullaby

Oh! hush thee, my baby, the night is behind us,
And black are the waters that sparkled so green.
The moon, o'er the combers, looks downward to find us
At rest in the hollows that rustle between.
Where billow meets billow, there soft be thy pillow;
Ah, weary wee flipperling, curl at thy ease!
The storm shall not wake thee, nor shark overtake thee,
Asleep in the arms of the slow-swinging seas.

Rudyard Kipling

Seal

See how he dives
From the rooks with a zoom!
See how he darts
Through his watery room
Past crabs and eels
And green seaweed,
Past fluffs of sandy
Minnow feed!
See how he swims
With a swerve and a twist,
A flip of the flipper,
A flick of the wrist!
Quicksilver-quick,
Softer than spray,
Down he plunges
And sweeps away;
Before you can think,
Before you can utter
Words like 'Dill pickle'
Or 'Apple Butter',
Back up he swims
Past sting ray and shark,
Out with a zoom,
A whoop, a bark;
Before you can say
Whatever you wish,
He plops at your side
With a mouthful of fish!

William Jay Smith

Whale

Wouldn't you like to be a whale
And sail serenely by—
An eighty-foot whale from your tip to your tail
And a tiny, briny eye?
Wouldn't you like to wallow
Where nobody says 'Come out!'?
Wouldn't you *love* to swallow
And blow all the brine about?
Wouldn't you like to be always clean
But never have to wash, I mean,
And wouldn't you love to spout—
 O yes, just think—
A feather of spray as you sail away,
And rise and sink and rise and sink,
And blow all the brine about?

Geoffrey Dearmer

The whale skeleton that has hung from the ceiling of Hintze Hall since 2017 has been named Hope because the blue whale – the largest animal ever known – was on the verge of extinction before the International Whaling Commission began work to protect these giants of the ocean. Hope was a female over twenty-five metres long who was beached on the Irish coast in 1891. Her heart would have been the size of a car, and her arteries like drainpipes.

The model blue whale is the crowning glory of the Mammals galleries. It's around thirty metres long and was constructed on site with plaster of Paris over a wooden frame in 1938, and was based on whales that had been washed up. We now know – thanks to sophisticated underwater photography – that they are shaped a little differently, but the model still gives a real sense of the immense scale of these animals.

Staff posing with blue whale model, 1938

Whale

We discussed
when and where whales sleep
(if they even do). How heavy
is a whale's dream? Maybe it can
only dream once a century. All the rest
of its wide-lipped, big-jawed,
muscle-turned, blink-free day – it fits in,
before tackling its first wink,
its first breath, and its last.
Who could stop a whale doing that?

Its swimming is a graceful egg, a perfect
bowl of white lilies, the pure sound
of a Ming vase.
It does not swim, but pipes the ocean
through its veins, once a day –
turns it in one almighty somersault,
straight up, straight over.
The globe, an aristocrat of acrobats,
is a safe tennis ball in its mouth,
spinning effortlessly – taking
its first breath in with its last,
one long slow breath
before the whale can dream again,
before the Earth should chance to cool –
to spin, to stop.

Helen Burke

Lizards, from Dr Hermann Burmeister's Atlas (1835)

'How doth the little crocodile /
Improve his shining tail' – Reptiles

Some of the most ancient, endangered and fascinating creatures on earth are cold-blooded. The Natural History Museum's collections of reptile and amphibian specimens is one of the oldest in the world, dating back to the eighteenth century. It includes around 200,000 items including skins, skulls and skeletons, fluid-preserved and taxidermy specimens and detailed models.

Among the highlights are a huge crocodile with its stomach still full of its last meal, a snake halfway through swallowing an egg and a tadpole three times the size of the frog it will eventually become. Visitors can also peek inside a tortoise's shell and see an unusual frog with fur.

A Narrow Fellow

A narrow fellow in the grass
Occasionally rides;
You may have met him, – did you not?
His notice sudden is.

The grass divides as with a comb,
A spotted shaft is seen;
And then it closes at your feet
And opens further on.

He likes a boggy acre,
A floor too cool for corn.
Yet when a child, and barefoot,
I more than once at morn,

Have passed, I thought, a whip-lash
Unbraiding in the sun, –
When stooping to secure it,
It wrinkled, and was gone.

Several of nature's people
I know, and they know me;
I feel for them a transport
Of cordiality;

But never met this fellow,
Attended or alone,
Without a tighter breathing,
And zero at the bone.

Emily Dickinson

Adder

A hank of rope in the late hot sun; a curl
of bark; a six, an eight:
For adder is as adder basks.

Deep in heather, coiled in gorse, sunk among
the winter stones:
For adder is as adder hides.

Darts, diamond slides, sine-wave swerves,
live-wire curves of force:
For adder is as adder glides.

Echo of snake, self-escape, a left-behind ghost:
For adder is as adder sheds.

Rustle of grass, sudden susurrus, what
the eye misses:
For adder is as adder hisses.

Robert Macfarlane

So small?

and now someone has seen
the teeniest lizard there's ever been
in existence, a gecko smaller
than my baby sister's finger

and I'm wondering
if somewhere there could be
herds of tiny elephants,
giraffes and hippopotamus browsing

a grassy clearing in a forest
where sunlight washes over a splash
of green water and on the edge
thumb-size crocodiles snooze

while among the plants and shrubs
mini-geckos flicker elastic tongues,
catch flies that cloud the air
like specks of dust.

Joan Poulson

Lizard

A lean wizard—
watch me slither
up and down
the breadfruit tree
sometimes pausing a while
for a dither in the sunshine

The only thing
that puts a jitter up my spine
is when I think about
my great great great
great great great great
great great grandmother
Dinosaura Diplodocus

She would have the shock of her life
if she were to come back
and see me reduced to lizardsize!

Grace Nichols

Lizard

A flash of green,
a flicker of light,
a gleam of gold
  glittering
just out of sight.

A heat-hazed wall,
a wreath of vine,
a glint of eye
  blinking
in bright sunshine.

A zap of speed,
a glimmer of jade,
a hint of movement
  diving
deep into shade.

Moira Andrew

The Pond

Now it seems
like a dream
that June afternoon
when we found
the pond
by the path.

And the pond
was alive, brimful.
bristling, wriggling
with brand new life.

And you cupped
your hands,
skimmed through
the water,
as one little tickler
twitched in your palm;
a blob for a body
and a pointy tail,
so black, like soot,
like a miniature whale:
such a restless soul
is a tadpole.

James Carter

Toad

Stop looking like a purse. How could a purse
squeeze under the rickety door and sit,
full of satisfaction, in a man's house?

You clamber towards me on your four corners –
right hand, left foot, left hand, right foot.

I love you for being a toad,
for crawling like a Japanese wrestler,
and for not being frightened.

I put you in my purse hand, not shutting it,
and set you down outside directly under
every star.

A jewel in your head? Toad,
you've put one in mine,
a tiny radiance in a dark place.

Norman MacCaig

The Crocodile

How doth the little crocodile
   Improve his shining tail,
And pour the waters of the Nile
   On every golden scale!

How cheerfully he seems to grin,
   How neatly spreads his claws,
And welcomes little fishes in
   With gently smiling jaws!

Lewis Carroll

Crick, crack, crocodile!

Crick, crack, crocodile,
what bright shiny teeth,
what a fierce, dark smile.

I wouldn't like to meet you
when you're hungry or sad.
I'd shout: *Mr Crocodile,*
I taste very bad.

But I'd be glad to see you
in your jungle, by the river –
strong tail, scaley back,
handsome water-dragon.

Crick, crack, crick, crack, **snap!**

Joan Poulson

The Axolotl

You are the Peter Pan
Of the silent world
Where secret rivers flow
Through hidden caves,
And sinister rocks stare
With hollow eyes.

You flutter the pale wings
Of your gills
And gaze at your own
Never Land,
While bats rise like lost children
And stalactites loom
Like the sails of tall ships.

Brave Axolotl
With your eyes full of dreams,
I wish I could be like you
And never grow up,
Never grow up.

Clare Bevan

Tortoise Family Connections

On he goes, the little one,
Bud of the universe,
Pediment of life.

Setting off somewhere, apparently.
Whither away, brisk egg?

His mother deposited him on the soil as if he were no more than droppings,
And now he scuffles tinily past her as if she were an old rusty tin.

A mere obstacle,
He veers round the slow great mound of her—
Tortoises always foresee obstacles.

It is no use my saying to him in an emotional voice:
"This is your Mother, she laid you when you were an egg."

He does not even trouble to answer: "Woman, what have I to do with thee?"
He wearily looks the other way,
And she even more wearily looks another way still,
Each with the utmost apathy,
Incognisant,
Unaware,
Nothing.

As for papa,
He snaps when I offer him his offspring,
Just as he snaps when I poke a bit of stick at him,

Because he is irascible this morning, an irascible tortoise
Being touched with love, and devoid of fatherliness.

Father and mother,
And three little brothers,
And all rambling aimless, like little perambulating pebbles
   scattered in the garden,
Not knowing each other from bits of earth or old tins.

Except that papa and mama are old acquaintances, of course,
Though family feeling there is none, not even the beginnings.

Fatherless, motherless, brotherless, sisterless
Little tortoise.

Row on then, small pebble,
Over the clods of the autumn, wind-chilled sunshine,
Young gaiety.

Does he look for a companion?

No, no, don't think it.
He doesn't know he is alone;
Isolation is his birthright,
This atom.

To row forward, and reach himself tall on spiny toes,
To travel, to burrow into a little loose earth, afraid of the night,
To crop a little substance,
To move, and to be quite sure that he is moving:

Basta!
To be a tortoise!
Think of it, in a garden of inert clods
A brisk, brindled little tortoise, all to himself—
Adam!

In a garden of pebbles and insects
To roam, and feel the slow heart beat
Tortoise-wise, the first bell sounding
From the warm blood, in the dark-creation morning.

Moving, and being himself,
Slow, and unquestioned,
And inordinately there, O stoic!
Wandering in the slow triumph of his own existence,
Ringing the soundless bell of his presence in chaos,
And biting the frail grass arrogantly,
Decidedly arrogantly.

D. H. Lawrence

The oldest known giant tortoise can be found at the Natural History Museum. It's thought to have been between 200 and 250 years old and its life is particularly well documented, since it lived most of it at an army barracks in Mauritius after being brought there – probably from the Seychelles – in 1766. It's been suggested that a scar on its side is from a gunshot, but in fact this hardy animal died in 1918 after falling down a well.

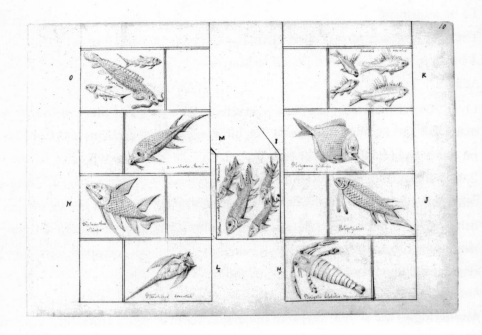

Sea Creatures

Designs for interior decorations of the Natural History Museum, London
Alfred Waterhouse, 1870s

'Sea Shell, Sea Shell' – Oceans and Rivers

Over 70% of the planet's surface is covered by the sea, and there are nearly as many fish species alive today as all the birds, reptiles, amphibians and mammals on earth combined. Some of the denizens of the deep sea who live between 2,000 and 5,000 metres below the surface are very peculiar indeed. Among other wonders, visitors to the Museum can see an example of a female football fish, which would have attracted her prey with a luminescent lantern dangling from their head. The collections also include sea urchins, octopuses, molluscs, crustaceans, sponges, worms and rare and beautiful corals.

Marine scientists at the Museum study specimens ranging from tiny, ancient fossils to enormous whale skeletons in order to find out more about our oceans. Their work contributes to vital debates about climate change, conservation and the impact of plastics, pollution and intensive fishing on our seas.

Turtle Beach

In the quiet of the evening
When the beach is long deserted,
While the moon is shining brightly
And the sand lies softly dreaming,
Under cover of the darkness
See the coming of the turtles,
Leaving their familiar waters,
Crawling up the beach in hundreds,
Digging holes above the tideline,
Flippers delving ever deeper,
Gently nesting in the moonlight,
Laying eggs in secret chambers.
Then the turtle mothers turning
Haul their heavy bodies seaward,
Back towards the pounding breakers
And the comfort of the ocean.

Sue Cowling

By The Sea

Why does the sea moan evermore?
      Shut out from heaven it makes its moan,
It frets against the boundary shore;
      All earth's full rivers cannot fill
      The sea, that drinking thirsteth still.

Sheer miracles of loveliness
      Lie hid in its unlooked-on bed:
Anemones, salt, passionless,
      Blow flower-like; just enough alive
      To blow and multiply and thrive.

Shells quaint with curve, or spot, or spike,
      Encrusted live things argus-eyed,
All fair alike, yet all unlike,
      Are born without a pang, and die
      Without a pang, and so pass by.

Christina Rossetti

Sea Shell

Sea Shell, Sea Shell,
Sing me a song, O Please!
A song of ships and pirate men,
And parrots, and tropical trees.

Of islands lost in the Spanish Main
Which no man may ever find again,
Of fishes and corals under the waves,
And sea-horses stabled in great green caves.

Sea Shell, Sea Shell,
Sing of the things you know so well.

Amy Lowell

Seashell

Shell at my ear –
come share how I hear
busy old sea in whispers.

Moans rise from ancient depths
in ocean sighs
like crowds of ghost monsters.

Waves lash and fall –
in roars and squalls
with all a mystery ahhh!

James Berry

A Green Crab's Shell

Not, exactly, green:
closer to bronze
preserved in kind brine,

something retrieved
from a Greco-Roman wreck,
patinated and oddly

muscular. We cannot
know what his fantastic
legs were like –

though evidence
suggests eight
complexly folded

scuttling works
of armament, crowned
by the foreclaws'

gesture of menace
and power. A gull's
gobbled the center,

leaving this chamber
– size of a demitasse –
open to reveal

a shocking, Giotto blue,
Though it smells
of seaweed and ruin,

this little traveling case
comes with such lavish lining!
Imagine breathing

surrounded by
the brilliant rinse
of summer's firmament.

What color is
the underside of skin?
Not so bad, to die,

if we could be opened
into *this* –
if the smallest chambers

of ourselves,
similarly,
revealed some sky.

Mark Doty

Lobster

Inside my slatey shell, blue-black as ink
I sink into green water.
Armoured like a knight
With spike and saw of crack-bone claw
I choose not to fight –
Prefer the quiet of holes,
The sea shadow of tall rocks
Where flocks of fish and shrimp shoals
Shiver pale and silver on slivers of stone.
In here I hunch,
Curl the crunch of my tough tail
Beneath me.
Stay still, unobserved,
Only my long antennae
Silently taste the moving tides
Receive the salty messages
Of the dark and secret sea.

Jan Dean

from **The Fish**

But there the night is close, and there
Darkness is cold and strange and bare;
And the secret deeps are whisperless;
And rhythm is all deliciousness;
And joy is in the throbbing tide,
Whose intricate fingers beat and glide
In felt bewildering harmonies
Of trembling touch; and music is
The exquisite knocking of the blood.
Space is no more, under the mud;
His bliss is older than the sun.
Silent and straight the waters run.
The lights, the cries, the willows dim,
And the dark tide are one with him.

Rupert Brooke

Minnows

Swarms of minnows show their little heads,
Staying their wavy bodies 'gainst the streams,
To taste the luxury of sunny beams
Tempered with coolness. How they ever wrestle
With their own sweet delight, and ever nestle
Their silver bellies on the pebbly sand.
If you but scantily hold out the hand,
That very instant not one will remain;
But turn your eye, and they are there again.

John Keats

The Pike

In the brown water,
Thick and silver-sheened in the sunshine,
Liquid and cool in the shade of the reeds,
A pike dozed.
Lost among the shadows of stems
He lay unnoticed.
Suddenly he flicked his tail,
And a green-and-copper brightness
Ran under the water.

Out from under the reeds
Came the olive-green light,
And orange flashed up
Through the sun-thickened water.
So the fish passed across the pool,
Green and copper,
A darkness and a gleam,
And the blurred reflections of the willows on the opposite bank
Received it.

Amy Lowell

The Loch Ness Monster's Song

Sssnnnwhufffll?

Hnwhuffl hhnnwfl hnfl hfl?

Gdroblboblhobngbl gbl gl g g g g glbgl.

Drublhaflablhaflubhafgabhaflhafl fl fl –

gm grawwwww grf grawf awfgm graw gm.

Hovoplodok – doplodovok – plovodokot-doplodokosh?

Splgraw fok fok splgrafhatchgabrlgabrl fok splfok!

Zgra kra gka fok!

Grof grawff gahf?

Gombl mbl bl –

blm plm,

blm plm,

blm plm,

blp.

Edwin Morgan

The Kraken

Below the thunders of the upper deep;
Far far beneath in the abysmal sea,
His ancient, dreamless, uninvited sleep
The Kraken sleepeth: faintest sunlights flee
About his shadowy sides: above him swell
Huge sponges of millennial growth and height;
And far away into the sickly light,
From many a wondrous grot and secret cell
Unnumber'd and enormous polypi
Winnow with giant fins the slumbering green.
There he hath lain for ages and will lie
Battening upon huge seaworms in his sleep,
Until the latter fire shall heat the deep;
Then once by men and angels to be seen,
In roaring he shall rise and on the surface die.

Alfred, Lord Tennyson

In the Museum's basement lurks 'Archie', a giant (female!) squid 8.62 metres long, preserved in a long tank. Giant squid live in every ocean though discovering whole specimens is so rare that for many centuries, people didn't know whether these monsters of the deep were real or mythical. Their eyes are the size of footballs, they have suckers filled with teeth and a strong beak, and their tissues contain ammonia which is released when they die. The team of excited curators preserving Archie had to do so enduring a very strong smell like urine.

The Museum also houses a tentacle from a colossal squid that was found in the stomach of a sperm whale. Its large suckers rotated into the flesh of its prey to grip it firmly. A fully grown colossal squid has never yet been found intact, but marine scientists believe they could grow to around eighteen metres long – longer than four cars.

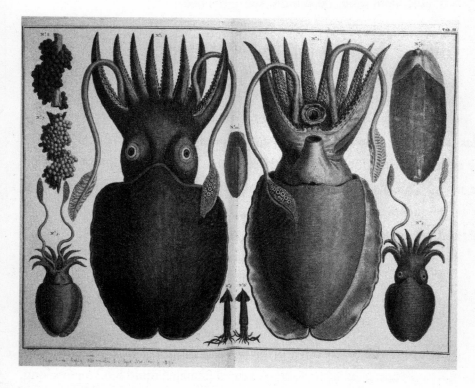

Squid illustration

Tableau 3 from Albertus Seba's Thesaurus, Vol 3, 1759.

The Octopus

Tell me, O Octopus, I begs,
Is those things arms, or is they legs?
I marvel at thee, Octopus;
If I were thou, I'd call me Us.

Ogden Nash

The Museum holds a beautiful collection of intricate marine creatures fashioned in glass during the nineteenth century by Leopold Blaschka and his son Rudolf. They are extraordinarily detailed and accurate – but we don't know how they were made. The Blaschkas worked alone and when they died, the secrets of their techniques were lost forever. Among the models are octopuses, jellyfish, corals and sea anemones.

The Lost Angels

In a fish tank in France
we discovered the lost angels,
fallen from heaven and floating now
on imaginary tides.
And all along the sides of the tank,
faces peered, leered at them,
laughing, pouting,
pointing, shouting,
while hung above their heads, a sign,
'Ne pas plonger les mains dans le bassin,'
Don't put your hands in the tank
-the turtles bite seriously.
And who can blame them,
these creatures with angels wings,
drifting past like alien craft.
Who knows what signals they send
through an imitation ocean,
out of sight of sky,
out of touch with stars?

Dream on, lost angels,
then one day, one glorious day,
you'll flap your wings
and fly again.

Brian Moses

Manta Ray

manta ray
breath of sea
wing-tips whisper
mystery

ocean shadow
floating kite
somersaulting
hood of night

Matt Goodfellow

Dolphin Dance

We are darters and divers
from secret sea-caves.
We're divers and gliders,
we dance through the waves.

We spiral and curl,
we weave as we fly,
stitch shimmering arches
from ocean to sky.

Judith Nicholls

The Maldive Shark

About the Shark, phlegmatical one,
Pale sot of the Maldive sea,
The sleek little pilot-fish, azure and slim,
How alert in attendance be.
From his saw-pit of mouth, from his charnel of maw,
They have nothing of harm to dread,
But liquidly glide on his ghastly flank
Or before his Gorgonian head;
Or lurk in the port of serrated teeth
In white triple tiers of glittering gates,
And there find a haven when peril's abroad,
An asylum in jaws of the Fates!

They are friends; and friendly they guide him to prey,
Yet never partake of the treat—
Eyes and brains to the dotard lethargic and dull,
Pale ravener of horrible meat.

Herman Melville

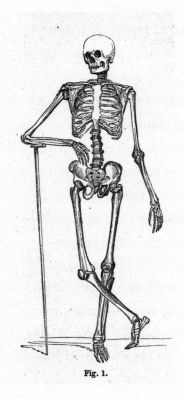

Fig. 1.

Human skeleton, from The Animal
Kingdom by Baron Cuvier (1849)

'Our footprints' – Human Evolution and Biology

In the Museum, visitors can explore the wonders of human evolution. They can also come face to face with our ancestors in the form of a scientifically accurate waxwork of a Neanderthal man and the first ever Neanderthal skull to be discovered, thought to be around 50,000 years old and once studied by Charles Darwin himself. One of our closest ancestors, Neanderthals are thought to have died out around 40,000 years ago, perhaps due to changes in climate and competition from another hominid species – us.

The Museum also houses the remains of Cheddar Man, a thousand-year-old skeleton discovered in 1903, and a reconstruction of his head. DNA extracted from Cheddar Man has given us a good idea of what he would have looked like, and we now believe he would have had dark skin and blue eyes.

Remembered More for His Beard Now

Remembered more for his beard now,
Bushy and white.
A touch of Father Christmas
On a face as stem as sandpaper
Taking no prisoners.
Never young.

Misremembered as having stated
That Man is descended from apes,
Causing some to query
Why it is
That the mating pair of gorillas
At the Royal Zoological Gardens
Has yet to give birth to
A young accountant.

When reminded that his actual conclusion is that
We share a common ancestry with apes,
There is outrage in SW19,
Where the only thing 'common' about them,
Or so they claim,
Is to be found as a patch of greenery in Wimbledon
(Since overrun with Wombles).

Reviled by those of faith,
Or those who hide behind it,
Darwin is also needled by those scientists
Who question his assertion as to

The Survival of the Fittest.
But soon his theories evolve into
The accepted norm,
Trampling detractors underfoot,
Their weak protestations taking one final, gasping breath.

When, at the behest of Her Majesty's Royal Mail,
His home village of Down
Evolves into Downe with a tail
In the form of a letter 'e',
Darwin stands firm.
His residence, Down House,
Remains unchanged.

Not unlike a dinosaur, with eyes tight shut,
A clawed finger in either ear; and humming loudly,
He attempts to postpone the inevitable,
Simply by denying that he can see it coming.
Yet Down House, with no e, it remains
To this day.

To the victor the spoils.

Closer inspection of Darwin's portraits reveals kind eyes.
Humanity amongst the facial hair,
Like the white-haired God of Sunday school.
Both worshipped by different congregations.
Forever and ever.
Charles Darwin.

Philip Ardagh

Mrs Darwin

7 April 1852.

Went to the Zoo.
I said to Him –
Something about that Chimpanzee over there reminds me of you.

Carol Ann Duffy

Charles Darwin (1809 – 1882)

Darwin's theories in the field of evolution revolutionized the way we understand the natural world. In 1831 he embarked on a five year voyage on board the *HMS Beagle*, exploring far-flung regions, collecting plant, animal and fossil specimens and making copious scientific notes.

The Natural History Museum houses many of those specimens and five pages of the notes Darwin wrote for his controversial instant bestseller *On The Origin of Species* (1859). In it, Darwin put forward his idea that the organisms best adapted to their environment are more likely to survive and breed, passing on their characteristics to the next generation. Gradually, these useful features would become more common and if the adaptations were dramatic enough, a new species could emerge. In a later book, *The Descent of Man*, he proposed the theory that human beings shared a common ancestor with apes.

Although his ideas met with resistance at the time, particularly from religious leaders because they questioned the biblical story of Creation, the book was published in many countries during Darwin's lifetime and his concepts are accepted by scientists as the most likely explanation for the amazing diversity of life found on earth.

Charles Darwin (1809-1882)

The Mushroom Hunters

Science, as you know, my little one, is the study
of the nature and behaviour of the universe.
It's based on observation, on experiment, and measurement,
and the formulation of laws to describe the facts revealed.

In the old times, they say, the men came already fitted with brains
designed to follow flesh-beasts at a run,
to hurdle blindly into the unknown,
and then to find their way back home when lost
with a slain antelope to carry between them.
Or, on bad hunting days, nothing.

The women, who did not need to run down prey,
had brains that spotted landmarks and made paths between them
left at the thorn bush and across the scree
and look down in the bole of the half-fallen tree,
because sometimes there are mushrooms.

Before the flint club, or flint butcher's tools,
The first tool of all was a sling for the baby
to keep our hands free
and something to put the berries and the mushrooms in,
the roots and the good leaves, the seeds and the crawlers.
Then a flint pestle to smash, to crush, to grind or break.

And sometimes men chased the beasts
into the deep woods,
and never came back.

Some mushrooms will kill you,
while some will show you gods
and some will feed the hunger in our bellies. Identify.

Others will kill us if we eat them raw,
and kill us again if we cook them once,
but if we boil them up in spring water, and pour the water away,
and then boil them once more, and pour the water away,
only then can we eat them safely. Observe.

Observe childbirth, measure the swell of bellies and the shape of breasts,
and through experience discover how to bring babies safely into the world.

Observe everything.

And the mushroom hunters walk the ways they walk
and watch the world, and see what they observe.
And some of them would thrive and lick their lips,
While others clutched their stomachs and expired.
So laws are made and handed down on what is safe. Formulate.

The tools we make to build our lives:
our clothes, our food, our path home . . .
all these things we base on observation,
on experiment, on measurement, on truth.

And science, you remember, is the study
of the nature and behaviour of the universe,
based on observation, experiment, and measurement,
and the formulation of laws to describe these facts.

The race continues. An early scientist
drew beasts upon the walls of caves
to show her children, now all fat on mushrooms
and on berries, what would be safe to hunt.

The men go running on after beasts.

The scientists walk more slowly, over to the brow of the hill
and down to the water's edge and past the place where the red clay runs.
They are carrying their babies in the slings they made,
freeing their hands to pick the mushrooms.

Neil Gaiman

The Caves

This is the cave of which I spoke,
These are the blackened stones, and these
Our footprints, seven lives ago.

Darkness was in the cave like shifting smoke,
Stalagmites grew like equatorial trees,
There was a pool, quite black and silent, seven lives ago.

Here such a one turned back, and there
Another stumbled and his nerve gave out;
Men have escaped blindly, they know not how.

Our candles gutter in the mouldering air,
Here the rock fell, beyond a doubt,
There was no light in those days, and there is none now.

Water drips from the roof, and the caves narrow,
Galleries lead downward to the unknown dark;
This was the point we reached, the farthest known.

Here someone in the debris found an arrow,
Men have been here before, and left their mark
Scratched on the limestone wall with splintered bone.

Here the dark word was said for memory's sake,
And lost, here on the cold sand, to the puzzled brow.

This was the farthest point, the fabled lake:
These were our footprints, seven lives ago.

Michael Roberts

Talking Hands

I've been thinking about those hands
    again. The ones on the walls in the caves
underground. And I'm wondering whether

they're warning - or waving - or simply
    just saying, *Hey, we were here too!*
It's easy for us. Thumbing our words

onto our phones and instantly pinging them
    out to the world. They only had paint,
and those cold, stone walls. Imagine

touching one of those hands. Just
    for an instant. Greeting an ancestor
lost in time with a simple high-five.

James Carter

Temptation

Call yourself alive? Look, I promise you
that for the first time you'll feel your pores opening
like fish mouths, and you'll actually be able to hear
your blood surging through all those lanes,
and you'll feel light gliding across the cornea
like the train of a dress. For the first time
you'll be aware of gravity
like a thorn in your heel,
and your shoulder blades will ache for want of wings.
Call yourself alive? I promise you
you'll be deafened by dust falling on the furniture,
you'll feel your eyebrows turning to two gashes,
and every memory you have – will begin
at Genesis.

Nina Cassian

translated from the Romanian by Brenda Walker & Andrea Deletant

fill your basket

for Violet

only so long
bones will be covered
by muscle, muscle
covered by flesh

only so long
limbs will be able to stretch
ears and throat
fill up with song

only so long
skin will be able to hold
a hug; a kiss; a caress

till then, let us cram
these baskets of body
with what life
we are lucky to get

Hollie McNish

Tempo

In the first month I think
it's a drop in a spider web's
necklace of dew

at the second a hazelnut; after,
a slim Black-eyed Susan demurely folded
asleep on a cloudy day

then a bushbaby silent as sap
in a jacaranda tree, but blinking
with mischief

at five months it's an almost-caught
flounder flapping back
to the glorious water

six, it's a song
with a chorus of basses: seven, five grapefruit
in a mesh bag that bounces on the hip
on a hot morning down at the shops

a watermelon next – green oval
of pink flesh and black seeds, ripe
waiting to be split by the knife

nine months it goes faster, it's a bicycle
pedalling for life over paddocks
of sun
no, a money-box filled with silver half-crowns

a sunflower following the clock
with its wide-open grin
a storm in the mountains, spinning rocks
down to the beech trees
three hundred feet below
– old outrageous Queen Bess's best dress
starched ruff and opulent tent of a skirt
packed with ruffles and lace
no no, I've remembered, it's a map
of intricate distinctions

purples for high ground burnt umber
for foothills green for the plains
and the staggering blue
of the ocean beyond
waiting and waiting and
aching
with waiting

no more alternatives! Suddenly now
you can see my small bag of eternity
pattern of power
my ace my adventure
my sweet-smelling atom
my planet, my grain of miraculous dust
my green leaf, my feather
my lily my lark
look at her, angels –
this is my daughter.

Lauris Edmond

Heredity

I am the family face;
Flesh perishes, I live on,
Projecting trait and trace
Through time to times anon,
And leaping from place to place
Over oblivion.

The years-heired feature that can
In curve and voice and eye
Despise the human span
Of durance – that is I;
The eternal thing in man,
That heeds no call to die.

Thomas Hardy

Traces

300 million years, and what remains of us?
      A gap, but oh,
so accurately mapped: the track
of one soft body in the seabed mud,
one mouth, with one thought: *eat*
        this? no, that? reaching
          to and fro

until it imprinted a frill in the silt
      reaching as far
as hunger can. Or here's the burrow
where it hid from jaw-snap and claw-nip
to slip out its feathery drift-net.
      What we truly touch
        we are.

Or here at the end of a trail
      that tracery as fine
as your hair. It's a snapshot in stone
of panic. Even a death-throe
at this distance is a message, a Last Will
      and Testament,
        a signed

confession, a love letter even,
in copperplate script,
posted under the door and – no! –
  it slipped
under the door mat of stone

that we crack open now
and . . . Look, who's it
        addressed to?

                Do you really want to know?

                              Philip Gross

Ichnologists: scientists who study traces such as burrows or footprints left by living things, sometimes preserved in ancient rocks as fossils.

Index of Poets

Index of First Lines

Acknowledgements

I'd like to thank every poet in this book, living and dead, for writing work so beautiful it enabled me to skulk along the sea bed, glide on wild winds, climb tall trees and even soar into space. The readers of this book, myself included, are so lucky to have you as guides to our beautiful universe. I'm so grateful to all the scientists, explorers, collectors, artists and thinkers who filled the halls of the Natural History Museum with such wonderful treasures, and everyone at the Museum who preserves them to inspire us.

Enormous thanks as always to my editor Gaby Morgan for this amazing opportunity, your attention and enthusiasm and all the poems you introduce me to. And three cheers for Tracey Ridgewell, Amy Boxshall and illustrator Melissa Castrillón for making this book so beautiful, for Charlie Castelletti for tirelessly hunting down permissions and for the Publicity and Marketing dream team Amber Ivatt and Charlie Morris for bringing the noise. A huge thank you to the sales team and all the amazing booksellers for putting the book into readers' hands.

I'd also like to thank my daughters Sophie and Laura for patiently listening to poems as I attempted to edit this book, work and homeschool you. We learned a lot about natural history, if little else!

Ana Sampson, 2021

The compiler and publisher would like to thank the following for permission to use their copyright material:

Al-Shabbi, Abu Al-Qassim: 'The Desire of Life' from *Modern Poetry in Translation, No 3 2020*, translated by Ali Al-Jamri, copyright © Ali Al-Jamri. Used with kind permission of the author; **Andrew, Moira:** 'Lizard', copyright © Moira Andrew. Used with kind permission of the author; **Ardagh, Philip:** 'Remembered More for His Beard Now' copyright © Philip Ardagh. Used with kind permission of the author; **Awolola, Ruth:** 'On Forgetting That I Am a Tree' from *Rising Stars* (Otter-Barry Press, 2017). Reproduced by kind permission of the author; **Belloc, Hilaire:** 'The Dodo' from *The Bad Child's Book of Beasts*; and *The Elephant* from *The Puffin Book of Funny Verse*. Reprinted by kind permission of Peters Fraser & Dunlop (www.petersfraserdunlop.com) on behalf of the Estate of Hilaire Belloc; **Benson, Gerard:** 'A Small Star' from *Wild.* Copyright © Gerard Benson. Used by kind permission on behalf of the estate of the author; **Berry, James:** 'Seashell' from *A Nestful of Stars* (Macmillan Children's Books, 2002) copyright © James Berry. Reprinted with the kind permission of the estate; **Berry, Wendell:** 'The Peace of Wild Things' from *New Collected Poems*, copyright © Wendell Berry, 2012. Reprinted with the kind permission of The Permissions Company, LLC on behalf of Counterpoint Press, counterpointpress. com; **Bevan, Clare:** 'The Axolotl', copyright © Clare Bevan. Reproduced by kind permission of the author; **Brandon, Jo:** 'We are volcanoes' from *Cures* (Valley Press, 2021). Reproduced by kind permission of Valley Press; **Brownlee, Liz:** 'The Blackbird' copyright © Liz Brownlee. Reproduced by kind permission of the author; **Burn, Jane:** 'This Is How We Walked' copyright © Jane Burn. Reproduced by kind permission of the author; **Carter, James:** 'The Pond', 'Talking Hands', '*Who cares*', 'Have you ever' and 'Meeting An Astronaut' copyright © James Carter. Reproduced by kind permission of the author and the publisher; **Cassian, Nina:** 'Temptation' from *Life Sentence: Selected Poems* (Anvil Press, 1990). Reproduced by kind permission of Carcanet Press,

Manchester, UK; **Clanchy, Kate:** 'The Natural History Museum' from *Selected Poems* (Picador, 2014) copyright © Kate Clanchy. Reproduced by kind permission of the publisher; **Conlon, Dom:** 'The Way Planets Talk' and 'Moons' copyright © Dom Conlon. Reproduced by kind permission of the author; **Cookson, Paul:** 'Invisible Magicians' and 'The King of all the Dinosaurs' copyright © Paul Cookson. Reproduced by kind permission of the author; **Cowling, Sue:** 'Turtle Beach' Copyright © Sue Cowling. Reproduced by kind permission of the author; **Darling Robertson, Shauna:** 'Swallowed' Copyright © Shauna Darling Robertson. Reproduced by kind permission of the author; **Dean, Jan:** 'Remembering Mary', 'Jurassic Coast' and 'Lobster' copyright © Jan Dean. Reproduced by kind permission of the author; **Doolittle, Hilda:** 'Pear Tree' from *H. D. Poems*, © by the Estate of Hilda Doolittle. Reproduced by kind permission of Carcanet Press, Manchester, UK; **Doty, Mark:** 'A Green Crab's Shell' from *Atlantis* (Johnathan Cape, 1996) copyright © Mark Doty, 1996. Reproduced by kind permission of The Random House Group Limited; **Duffy, Carol Ann:** 'Mrs. Darwin' from *The World's Wife* (Picador, 1999) and 'Virgil's Bees' and 'Atlas' from *New Selected Poems* by Carol Ann Duffy. Published by Picador. Copyright © Carol Ann Duffy. Reproduced by kind permission of the author c/o Rogers, Coleridge & White Ltd., 20 Powis Mews, London W11 1JN; **Edmond, Lauris:** 'Tempo' copyright © Lauris Edmonds. Reproduced by kind permission on behalf of the estate of the author; **Edwards, Richard:** 'Badgers' from *The Word Party* ed Richard Edwards (Lutterworth Press, 1985). Reproduced by kind permission of Johnson & Alcock, www.johnsonandalcock.co.uk; **Finney, Eric:** 'Finding Magic' from *I am the Seed*, copyright © Eric Finney. Reproduced by the kind permission of the Estate of the author; **Frost, Robert:** 'Fireflies in the Garden' from *The Poetry of Robert Frost*, edited by Edward Connery Lathem, copyright © Henry Holt and Company, Inc. 1928, 1969, renewed © 1956 by Robert Frost. Reprinted with the kind permission of The Random House Group Limited, and Henry Holt and Company. All rights reserved; **Gagnier, Camille:** 'Dinosaur Sonnet' copyright

author; **McGarry, Jamie:** 'A Snail's Advice to His Son' from *Dead Snail Diaries*, The Emma Press. Reproduced by kind permission of the author; **McNish, Hollie:** 'fill your basket' from *Slug*, (Fleet, 2021). Copyright © Hollie McNish, 2021. Reproduced by kind permission of Little, Brown Book Group; **Mitchell, Adrian:** 'Gorillas' and 'Elephant Eternity' by Adrian Mitchell from *Balloon Lagoon*, Orchard Books, 1997. Reproduced by kind permission of United Agents; **Mitchell, Elma:** 'Life-cycle of the Moth', from *The Human Cage* (Peterloo Poets, 1979) Copyright © Elma Mitchell. **Morgan, Edwin:** 'The Loch Ness Monster's Song' from *Collected Poems* (Carcanet Press, 1997) by Edwin Morgan. Copyright © Edwin Morgan. Reproduced by kind permission of Carcanet Press, Manchester, UK; **Morgan, Michaela:** 'Behind the Scenes at the Museum' and 'She Finds Fossils' copyright © Michaela Morgan. Reproduced by kind permission of the author; **Moses, Brian:** 'The Lost Angels' Copyright © Brian Moses. Used with kind permission of the author; **Mucha, Laura:** 'Dear Egg', 'Listening to' and 'Apatosaurus Rap' copyright © Laura Mucha. Reproduced by kind permission of David Higham Associates; **Nash, Ogden:** 'The Octopus', copyright © Ogden Nash, 1942, renewed. Reproduced by kind permission of Curtis Brown, Ltd; **Nicholas, Rachael:** 'A Real Live Fossil' Copyright © Rachael Nicholas. Reproduced by kind permission of the author; **Nicholls, Judith:** 'Cockroach' and 'Monkey', copyright © Judith Nicholls 1994 from *Storm's Eye* (Oxford University Press, 1994) and reprinted by kind permission of the author; 'Dolphin Dance' from *Caliban's Cave* (HarperCollins, 2011) copyright © Judith Nicholls, reprinted by kind permission of the author; **Nichols, Grace:** 'Cosmic Disco' written by Grace Nichols and illustrated by Alice Wright, published by Frances Lincoln Children's Book, an imprint of The Quarto Group, copyright © 2013. Reproduced by kind permission of Quarto Publishing Plc; 'Lizard' from *Come On Into My Tropical Garden*, 1988. Copyright © Grace Nichols, 1988. Reproduced with kind permission of Curtis Brown Ltd on behalf of Grace Nichols; **Oswald, Alice:** 'Excursion to the Planet Mercury' from *Woods etc.* (Faber, 2011) copyright © Alice Oswald. Reproduced by kind permission of Faber & Faber Ltd; **Paech, Neil:** 'Parrots'. Reproduced by kind permission of Wakefield Press; **Pearson, Cheryl:** 'Owl Poem' and 'Kronosaurus'. Copyright © Cheryl Pearson. Used with kind permission of the author; **Perry, Rebecca:** 'Dear Stegosaurus' from *Beauty/Beauty* (Bloodaxe Books, 2015) copyright © Rebecca Perry. Reproduced with kind permission of Bloodaxe Books; **Petit, Pascale:** 'Green Bee-eater', 'Indian Paradise Flycatcher' and '#ExtinctionRebellion' from *Tiger Girl* (Bloodaxe Books, 2020) copyright © Pascale Petit. Reproduced with kind permission of Bloodaxe Books; **Plath, Sylvia:** 'Mushrooms' from *Collected Poems*, Faber & Faber Ltd, 2002. Reproduced by kind permission of the Faber & Faber Ltd; **Poulson, Joan:** 'Crick, crack, crocodile!' and 'So small?' copyright © Joan Poulson. Used by kind permission of the author; **Pratt, Wendy:** 'Gryphaea' from *Museum Pieces*. Reproduced by kind permission of the author; **Ralleigh, Gita:** 'The Terror-Dragon's Thighbone' and 'Solar System Candy'. Copyright © Gita Ralleigh. Used with kind permission of the author; **Roethke, Theodore:** 'The Sloth' from *Collected Poems* by Theodore Roethke, Faber & Faber Ltd, copyright © Theodore Roethke, 1950, © 1966, renewed 1994 by Beatrice Lushington. Reproduced by kind permission of the publisher; and Doubleday, an imprint of the Knopf Doubleday Publishing Group, a division of Penguin Random House LLC. All rights reserved; **Simpson, Louis:** 'The Redwoods' from *The Owner of the House: New Collected Poems 1940-2001,* copyright © Louis Simpson, 1963, 2001. Reprinted with the kind permission of The Permissions Company, LLC on behalf of BOA Editions, Ltd., boaeditions.org; **Smith, William Jay:** 'Lion' from *Collected Poems 1939-1989*, Charles Scribner & Sons, copyright © William Jay Smith, 1990; and 'Seal' from *Boy Blue's Book of Beasts,* Atlantic-Little, Brown & Co, copyright © William Jay Smith, 1957. Reproduced by kind permission of the Estate of William Jay Smith; **Steven, Kenneth C:** 'Grey Geese' by Kenneth C. Steven. Copyright © Kenneth C. Steven. Used with kind permission of the author; **Tempest, Kae:** 'And as we followed dinosaurs' from *Hold Your Own* (Picador, 2014) © Kae Tempest, granted with kind permission of

Lewinsohn Literary Agency Ltd; 'Let Them Eat Chaos' copyright © Kae Tempest. Used with kind permission of the publisher; **Thomas, Dylan:** 'Being but men' from *The Collected Poems of Dylan Thomas* (Weidenfeld & Nicolson, 2014). Copyright © Dylan Thomas Trust. Used with kind permission of David Higham Associates on behalf of the estate of the author; **Toczek, Nick:** 'Beast' Copyright © Nick Toczek. Used with kind permission of the author; **Towers, Katharine:** 'The Grasshopper' from *The Remedies* (Picador, 2016). Copyright © Katharine Towers. Used with kind permission of the publisher; **Wakeling, Kate:** 'Comet' Copyright © Kate Wakeling. Used with kind permission of the author; **Walton, Rob:** 'Velociraptors' Copyright © Rob Walton. Used with kind permission of the author; **Warren, Celia:** 'Crinoid Fossils'. Copyright © Celia Warren 2021. Used with kind permission of the author; **Weil, Zaro:** 'Think of it' Copyright © Zaro Weil. Used with kind permission of the author; **Williams, Kate:** 'Butterfly' Copyright © Kate Williams. Used with kind permission of the author; **Woollard, Elli:** 'Dinosaurs Walked Here'. Copyright © Elli Woollard. Used with kind permission of the author.

Image credits

Central Hall of the Natural History Museum, London xvi, Wold meteorite landing site p22, Interior view of the crater of Mount Vesuvius p44, *Quercus rober niger*, oak tree p52, Designs for the Natural History Museum, by Alfred Waterhouse (1830-1905) p75, *Stegosaurus stenops* p76, *Diplodocus* skeleton p81, Mary Anning (1799-1847) p88, *Bubo virginianus*, great-horned owl p106, *Nymphicus hollandicus*, cockatiel p125, *Raphus cucullatus*, Dodo p133, Plate XXVI, The Green Fly p134, Plate XXI, The Unicorn p145, Flossenfusser – Pinniped (Seal) p158, *Ornithorhynchus anatinus*, duck-billed platypus p175, Staff posing with blue whale model, 1938 p179, Burmeister's Atlas p182, Sea Creatures p198, Squid illustration p213, Human skeleton p220, Museum Poster from Darwin: Big Idea Exhibition p226, A detail of the South Elevation of the Natural History Museum, end-papers.

SOUTH E

Drawing of the South Elevation of the new Natural History Museum building

Alfred Waterhouse, 9th February 1872